Serenity at Sunset

100 Most Powerful Prayers to Soothe the Soul

Evening Prayers

Find Serenity and Inner Peace with Prayers Before Bedtime

Honor Wells

For permission requests, please contact the publisher at TheSoaringMinds@gmail.com

Published by The Soaring Minds
Printed in USA

Introduction

Welcome to "Serenity at Sunset: 100 Most Powerful Evening Prayers to Soothe the Soul." In the tranquility of twilight, as the sun dips below the horizon, it is the perfect time to find solace, seek inner peace, and connect with the divine. This prayer book is a gentle companion designed to guide you on a serene journey towards a calm and restful night.

This book is crafted to be a source of comfort and inspiration as you wind down your day and prepare for a peaceful night's sleep. Each prayer within these pages has been carefully selected to touch your heart, ease your mind, and nourish your soul. Whether you choose to read a single prayer or indulge in several, take a moment to immerse yourself in its words and let its gentle power embrace you.

To get the most out of this book, find a quiet and serene space where you can immerse yourself in prayer without distraction. You may choose to read a prayer aloud or silently, allowing the words to resonate within your being. Engage all your senses and let the peace and tranquility of the evening envelop you.

"Serenity at Sunset" is intended for anyone who seeks solace, inner peace, and a deeper connection with the divine. If you long for moments of serenity in your busy life, if you desire to quiet the noise of the world and find stillness within, this book is for you. It is a gentle invitation to those seeking to establish a nightly ritual of spiritual nourishment, to those yearning to release the burdens of the day, and to those who wish to embrace the power of prayer before drifting into peaceful slumber.

Whether you are new to the practice of prayer or have a well-established spiritual routine, "Serenity at Sunset" offers a variety of prayers that speak to the human experience. It transcends religious boundaries, appealing to individuals from all walks of life who seek solace and find comfort in the sacred moments of the evening.

May these 100 most powerful evening prayers become a cherished companion on your journey towards serenity and inner peace. As you embrace the tranquility of the sunset, may your soul find solace, and may your heart be filled with gratitude and love.

Wishing you peaceful evenings and restful nights,
Honor Wells.

Dear Reader,

We invite you to share your thoughts and experiences by leaving a review for our book, " Serenity at Sunset: 100 Most Powerful Evening Prayers to Soothe the Soul" on Amazon. As a small independent publisher, we greatly value your feedback and appreciate your support in spreading the word about our work.

Your honest review not only helps other readers make informed decisions but also plays a significant role in the success of independent authors like us. We believe that your unique perspective will add depth to the conversation surrounding this book and contribute to a community of spiritual seekers.

Whether you found solace in the evening prayers, discovered a renewed sense of purpose, or resonated with the themes of love, forgiveness, and inner peace, we would love to hear from you. Your review will not only be a testament to the book's impact but also a source of encouragement for our future endeavors.

Thank you for taking the time to share your thoughts and for supporting independent publishing. We are immensely grateful for your support and look forward to hearing your insights.

With heartfelt appreciation,

Honor Wells

The Soaring Minds

Scan the QR Code below to write a review.
(It only takes 60 seconds)

Table of Contents

GUIDANCE

STRENGTH

PEACE

HEALING

REFLECTION

UNITY

HOPE

FAITH

COMPASSION

LETTING GO

GRACIOUSNESS

CONTENTMENT

RENEWAL

CONNECTION

CLARITY

SAFETY

GRATITUDE

<u>Prayer 1: Daily Provision</u>

Giving thanks for the basic necessities of life, such as food, shelter, and safety that were provided throughout the day

In the twilight's gentle embrace, I kneel,
To offer a prayer, heartfelt and real,
For the provisions granted, day by day,
The sustenance that nourishes my way.

Oh, Divine Provider, hear my plea,
For the gift of sustenance bestowed on me,
For the bread that fills my hunger's call,
And the shelter that shields me from the squall.

For the meals that grace my table's expanse,
Nourishing my body, giving me a chance,
To thrive and flourish, to grow and soar,
I bow in gratitude, forevermore.

In the quiet sanctuary of the night,
I humbly beseech, with all my might,
Thank you for the warmth of a cozy bed,
Where I lay my weary soul to rest my head.

For the roof that shelters from wind and rain,
Grant me strength to never take in vain,
The refuge provided, a safe retreat,
Where dreams are nurtured, in slumber sweet.

Oh, Divine Guardian, I implore,
Keep me safe from harm, forevermore,
For the safety and security you bestow,
I'm forever grateful, this I humbly show.

As I close my eyes in this tranquil hour,
Grant me the wisdom and the power,
To cherish the blessings you freely give,
And with gratitude, each day, to live.

In this evening prayer, I truly yearn,
To express my thanks, to deeply discern,
That the daily provisions I receive,
Are gifts from You, in whom I believe.

So, I offer this plea, with heartfelt zeal,
Grateful for the blessings that are so real,
For the basic necessities, I will adore,
And cherish them always, forevermore.

GRATITUDE

Prayer 2: Relationships

Expressing gratitude for the love, support, companionship received from family, friends, and other meaningful connections.

In the twilight's sacred glow, I kneel and pray,
To honor the bonds that brighten my way,
For the cherished souls, in my life so dear,
Whose love and support bring me joy and cheer.

Oh, Divine Creator, hear my plea,
For the gift of relationships bestowed on me,
For family's embrace, a haven of love,
And friendships that soar, like wings of a dove.

For the laughter shared, and tears wiped away,
For the comfort and solace, day after day,
I beg of you, let these connections remain strong,
And bless them with harmony, forever long.

In the depths of my heart, gratitude resides,
For the hands that hold mine through life's turbulent tides,
For the ears that listen, without judgment or disdain,
And the voices that soothe, in times of pain.

Oh, Divine Source of love and light,
Grant me the grace to cherish, with all my might,
The companionship that colors my days,
And ignites my spirit in countless ways.

For the friends who lift me when I'm feeling low,
Whose presence, like sunshine, makes my spirit glow,
I humbly ask, bless them abundantly,
With happiness, peace, and love eternally.

And for my family, the foundation of my soul,
Whose unwavering support has made me whole,
I bow before you, with heartfelt plea,
Keep them safe and surrounded by harmony.

In this evening prayer, I humbly implore,
That these relationships, forevermore,
Stay strong, resilient, and ever true,
With gratitude, I offer my thanks to you.

May the bonds we share grow deeper each day,
And may love and compassion forever light our way,
For the gift of relationships, I'm forever blessed,
And in gratitude, my soul finds rest.

GRATITUDE

Prayer 3: Opportunities

Being thankful for the opportunities that were presented during the day, whether it be for personal growth, learning, or new experiences

In the evening's hush, I kneel and pray,
Grateful for the chances that came my way,
For the doors swung open, opportunities bestowed,
For the moments that shaped me and helped me grow.

Oh, Divine Architect of fate and time,
In humble reverence, I seek the sublime,
For the opportunities that grace my path,
I beseech you, let them forever last.

For the lessons learned in trials faced,
For the wisdom gained through every embrace,
I plead with you, grant me discerning sight,
To seize opportunities, both small and bright.

In the tapestry of life, each thread a chance,
To learn, to create, to truly advance,
I implore you, guide me on this intricate thread,
So, I may embrace opportunities with a heart unfed.

For the encounters that broaden my view,
For the challenges that make me anew,
I humbly ask, let me see with clear eyes,
The opportunities that silently arise.

Oh, Divine Weaver of destinies untold,
I pray for opportunities, manifold,
To learn, to grow, to explore and create,
To embrace each chance, before it's too late.

In this evening prayer, I fervently yearn,
For the opportunities that I truly discern,
May they be abundant, diverse, and grand,
And may I grasp them with a determined hand.

For the doors opened wide, for new experiences sought,
For personal growth, with every lesson taught,
I kneel before you, in awe and in plea,
Grateful for the opportunities that set my spirit free.

GRATITUDE

Prayer 4: Lessons Learned

Showing gratitude for the lessons and insights gained from challenges, mistakes, or difficult moments encountered during the day

In the tranquil twilight's embrace, I kneel to pray,
To honor the lessons learned throughout the day,
For the challenges faced, mistakes made in stride,
I seek the wisdom within, where truth resides.

Oh, Divine Teacher, hear my humble plea,
For the blessings disguised in adversity,
For the lessons woven through trials and strife,
I beg of you, grant me clarity in this life.

For every stumble, every fall from grace,
For the scars that mark my spirit's embrace,
I implore you, guide me with your gentle hand,
To learn from my mistakes, to truly understand.

In the depths of my soul, I hold gratitude,
For the difficult moments, the hardships pursued,
For they mold and shape me, they carve my soul,
And grant me strength to achieve my ultimate goal.

Oh, Divine Alchemist, I plead for your grace,
To transform my trials into pearls of embrace,
For the wisdom gained, the insights deep and profound,
I bow before you, with heartfelt reverence profound.

For the mistakes made, the wrong turns taken,
For the path of growth that they have awakened,
I ask of you, illuminate my heart and mind,
With the light of understanding, patient and kind.

In this evening prayer, I yearn to express,
The gratitude for each lesson, for I confess,
That through challenges and failures, I truly see,
The opportunities for growth and the chance to be free.

Oh, Divine Guide, as the day comes to an end,
Let the lessons learned deeply descend,
Into my being, as seeds of wisdom and grace,
Nurturing my spirit, at my own pace.

For the lessons learned, both bitter and sweet,
I offer my thanks, with a heart complete,
May I embrace the teachings that unfold,
And carry their essence, as treasures untold.

In this evening prayer, with sincere plea,
I honor the lessons learned, so graciously,
Grant me the strength to embrace each day anew,
With gratitude for the lessons that bring me closer to you.

GRATITUDE

Prayer 5: Moments of Joy

Acknowledging and appreciating the moments of joy, beauty, and happiness experienced throughout the day, no matter how small or fleeting they may have been

In the gentle twilight's glow, I humbly bow,
To offer my prayer, with gratitude and vow,
For the moments of joy, however brief they may be,
I plead with you, let their essence forever stay with me.

Oh, Divine Creator, hear my fervent plea,
For the glimpses of beauty that set my spirit free,
For the moments of happiness that light up my soul,
I beg of you, let their memory forever console.

For the laughter that echoes in my heart's core,
For the smiles that bring solace when my spirit is sore,
I implore you, bless me with eyes that truly see,
The moments of joy, however small they may be.

In the tapestry of life, woven with joy and strife,
I seek solace in the moments that bring respite,
For the simple pleasures that brighten my day,
I beseech you, let them forever hold sway.

Oh, Divine Source of love and light,
Grant me the grace to appreciate, with all my might,
The moments of joy, however fleeting they may seem,
For they are the beacons that make my spirit gleam.

For the beauty of nature, in every sight and sound,
For the melodies that uplift and profound,
I humbly ask, let me savor each melody,
And find solace in the moments of harmony.

In this evening prayer, I plead and yearn,
For the moments of joy, I ardently discern,
May I cherish them deeply, hold them in my heart,
And let their essence guide me, never to depart.

For the moments of joy, a divine gift bestowed,
I offer my thanks, with a heart that's overflowed,
May they continue to bless my path every day,
And in their embrace, may I forever sway.

Oh, Divine Bestower of moments that bring delight,
Illuminate my soul with their radiant light,
In gratitude and awe, I offer this plea,
To forever cherish the moments of joy that grace me.

FORGIVENESS

Prayer 6: Personal Reflection

Taking time to reflect on one's actions and seeking forgiveness for any mistakes or wrongs committed during the day

In this quiet hour, I humbly bow my head,
To reflect upon my deeds, with words left unsaid.
For in the depths of my soul, I feel the weight,
Of mistakes and wrongs committed, a burden I can't abate.

O gracious Spirit, hear my heartfelt plea,
As I search within for truth and clarity.
Grant me the courage to face my flaws,
And the strength to seek forgiveness, by your divine laws.

In moments of haste, I may have caused pain,
Words spoken in anger, leaving scars, not wane.
I plead for forgiveness, for the harm I've done,
Grant me the wisdom to heal, to mend what's been undone.

With each passing day, I strive to be better,
To learn from my missteps, to grow and unfetter.
But there are times when I stumble and fall,
I implore your guidance, to rise above it all.

In this sacred space of introspection and grace,
I surrender my pride, with tears upon my face.
May my actions speak louder, as I seek to amend,
And in the embrace of forgiveness, find solace to transcend.

O Divine Light, illuminate my path so clear,
Grant me the grace to face my shadows without fear.
In this evening prayer, I seek absolution and release,
With a contrite heart, I plead for your mercy and peace.

Guide me towards compassion, towards a better way,
May personal reflection bring enlightenment today.
In your infinite wisdom, help me grow and evolve,
And in the journey of self-forgiveness, let me dissolve.

Through humble introspection, I seek to become whole,
May my evening prayers bring healing to my soul.
I pledge to learn from my mistakes and do what's right,
In your divine presence, I find solace every night.

FORGIVENESS

Prayer 7: Reconciliation

Praying for the restoration of broken relationships and seeking forgiveness from those who have been hurt or offended

In the stillness of this evening, I humbly come to You,
With a heart burdened by the pain of relationships askew.
Oh, Divine Redeemer, hear my earnest plea,
Grant me the grace of reconciliation, set my spirit free.

I seek your guidance, for bridges have been burned,
Words were spoken in anger, and hearts have yearned.
In the darkness of misunderstanding, love has been obscured,
I beseech you, bring forth healing, let forgiveness be assured.

Lord, soften the hearts that have grown hard,
Mend the bonds that have been torn apart and marred.
In this sacred hour, I humbly lay my pride aside,
With a repentant spirit, I ask for forgiveness far and wide.

Grant me the words to speak with empathy and care,
To seek reconciliation, for love to repair.
Help me to understand the pain I may have caused,
And to make amends, to reconcile the hearts that were once close.

In your boundless compassion, teach me the way,
To rebuild what's been broken, to let forgiveness sway.
May reconciliation flow like a gentle stream,
Restoring what was lost, making hearts gleam.

In this evening prayer, I plead for reconciliation's embrace,
To mend the wounds inflicted, with humility and grace.
Restore the broken relationships, let forgiveness bloom,
And in the bonds of love renewed, let us find our room.

Oh, Divine Healer, mend what is torn asunder,
Let reconciliation be a testament of your wonder.
May this plea for restoration be heard on high,
As we seek forgiveness and unity under your sky.

FORGIVENESS

Prayer 8: Self-Forgiveness

Seeking forgiveness and letting go of guilt for one's own shortcomings, mistakes, or failures

In the twilight's gentle glow, I kneel in humble plea,
Seeking solace and release, from burdens that burden me.
For within my weary heart, guilt and remorse reside,
I implore you, grant me self-forgiveness, let guilt subside.

Oh, Merciful One, I lay my shortcomings at your feet,
The mistakes I've made, the failures I've come to meet.
In the depths of my remorse, I long to find reprieve,
Grant me the grace to forgive myself, to believe.

The weight of guilt upon my soul has left me worn,
Regrets and shadows linger, causing my spirit to mourn.
I beg for your compassion, to heal my wounded heart,
To grant me the mercy to forgive and make a fresh start.

In the quiet of this evening, let redemption's light shine,
Release me from the shackles of guilt, that I may realign.
I seek the strength to face my flaws with honest eyes,
To embrace my imperfections, and let forgiveness arise.

Oh, Divine Light, guide me on this path of self-forgiveness,
Help me learn from the past, to live with greater consciousness.
With a contrite heart, I offer my shortcomings to your care,
Grant me the serenity to let go, the strength to repair.

In this sacred moment, I surrender my self-blame,
May self-forgiveness cleanse my soul, extinguishing the flame.
For in the depths of my being, I seek your sacred grace,
To find forgiveness within myself, in your loving embrace.

Oh, Loving Presence, hear my earnest plea tonight,
Grant me the courage to forgive myself, to set things right.
In the quietude of this evening, let healing waters flow,
And may self-forgiveness guide me towards inner glow.

As darkness falls and stars alight, I release the past's hold,
With gratitude for the lessons learned, my spirit is consoled.
In this evening prayer, I find solace in your love's embrace,
Grant me the strength to forgive myself, and to embrace your grace.

FORGIVENESS

Prayer 9: Forgiving Others

Praying for the ability to forgive others who have wronged or hurt us, releasing resentment and promoting reconciliation

In the stillness of this evening, I come before Your grace,
Seeking strength and courage to forgive and find embrace.
For within my wounded heart, resentment has taken hold,
I plead with You, grant me the power to forgive, let love unfold.

Oh, Divine Compassion, hear my earnest plea,
Release me from the chains of anger and enmity.
For those who have wronged me, I beseech Your guiding light,
Grant me the grace to forgive, to let go of the strife.

In the depths of hurt and pain, forgiveness seems so far,
But I implore Your mercy, to heal each bitter scar.
Grant me the wisdom to see beyond the harm that's been done,
To find compassion and understanding, to let forgiveness run.

I lay my grievances at Your feet, with a heavy heart,
I yearn for reconciliation, for a brand new start.
Grant me the strength to bridge the divide, to let forgiveness flow,
To mend the broken bonds, and let compassion grow.

Oh, Divine Love, I ask for the power to release,
The resentment that consumes me, that hinders inner peace.
In this sacred moment, I seek forgiveness from above,
To break the chains of resentment, and embrace forgiveness' love.

Guide me towards empathy, towards a heart that's free,
To see the humanity in those who've wronged me.
In this evening prayer, I plead for the ability to mend,
To forgive those who've hurt me, and find peace that will transcend.

As twilight fades and darkness claims the sky,
May forgiveness reign, letting bitterness pass by.
Grant me the courage to extend an olive branch in grace,
To forgive others as I seek forgiveness in this sacred space.

Oh, Divine Mercy, hear my plea, for forgiveness to abound,
For the healing of wounds and reconciliation to resound.
In this evening prayer, I release all resentment and strife,
Grant me the gift of forgiveness, and transform my life.

FORGIVENESS

Prayer 10: Inner Peace

Seeking forgiveness as a means to find inner peace and
harmony, allowing oneself to heal and move forward

In the stillness of this evening, I seek serenity divine,
To find solace in forgiveness, and let inner peace align.
With a humble heart, I lay my burdens at your feet,
Grant me the grace to forgive, to find harmony complete.

Oh, tranquil presence, hear my heartfelt plea,
I long for inner peace, for my spirit to be free.
Release me from the shackles of resentment and pain,
Grant me the courage to forgive, to let go and regain.

In the depths of my being, turmoil may reside,
But I implore your mercy, let forgiveness be my guide.
For in the act of pardoning, I find the path to heal,
To embrace inner peace, to let love's light reveal.

Grant me the strength to release the past's hold,
To forgive those who have hurt me, as my heart unfolds.
In this quiet hour, I surrender to your divine grace,
Let forgiveness mend my spirit, let inner peace replace.

Oh, soothing presence, wash away my inner strife,
Fill me with tranquility, and the balm of a forgiving life.
Grant me the wisdom to see beyond the pain,
To cultivate forgiveness and let inner peace reign.

In this evening prayer, I seek the serenity of heart,
To release the burdens that tear my soul apart.
Grant me the grace to forgive, to find solace deep within,
To let go of resentment, and let healing begin.

Oh, divine source of peace, envelop me in your embrace,
As forgiveness takes root, let inner turmoil erase.
Grant me the serenity to heal, to move forward with grace,
And in the realm of inner peace, find a sacred space.

As twilight casts its gentle glow, I surrender to your will,
Seeking forgiveness, finding solace, my heart begins to still.
In this evening prayer, I embrace forgiveness as my guide,
To cultivate inner peace and let love's essence reside.

FORGIVENESS

Prayer 11: Seeking Forgiveness

Praying for the strength and humility to seek forgiveness from others for any wrongs committed, whether intentional or unintentional

In the stillness of this evening, I humbly bow my head,
With a heavy heart, I seek forgiveness, my soul in need of thread.
For the words I've spoken, the actions I've done amiss,
I plead with you, grant me the courage to seek forgiveness.

Oh, Merciful One, I lay my faults before Your grace,
In this solemn hour, I seek redemption's embrace.
For the hurts I've caused, the pain I've unknowingly sown,
Grant me the strength to seek forgiveness, to make amends known.

With a contrite heart, I acknowledge my mistakes,
The wounds inflicted, the trust I've broken, for heaven's sake.
I yearn for reconciliation, for bridges to be restored,
Grant me the humility to seek forgiveness, to mend what's been ignored.

In this quietude of evening, I confront my shortcomings bold,
Seeking forgiveness from those I've hurt, my heart deeply behold.
Grant me the words to express my remorse and regret,
To acknowledge the pain I've caused, and seek forgiveness, lest I forget.

Oh, Divine Forgiver, hear my earnest plea,
To humble myself, to seek forgiveness on bended knee.
In this sacred moment, I let go of pride and ego's sway,
Grant me the grace to seek forgiveness, to pave the way.

In the twilight's gentle glow, I seek reconciliation's path,
To mend the broken bonds, to confront the aftermath.
Grant me the strength to face the consequences of my wrongs,
To seek forgiveness, to heal, and find where forgiveness belongs.

As the night unfolds its cloak, I implore You, guide my way,
Grant me the wisdom and courage to seek forgiveness each day.
May this prayer be heard, and forgiveness bestowed,
That I may mend the broken and lighten my heavy load.

FORGIVENESS

Prayer 12: Granting Forgiveness

Praying for the ability to extend forgiveness to those who have wronged us, releasing resentment and embracing a spirit of compassion

In the hush of this evening, I kneel in solemn prayer,
Seeking the strength to forgive, burdens I cannot bear.
For the pain inflicted upon me, the wounds that cut so deep,
I plead with You, grant me the power to forgive, to let resentment seep.

Oh, Divine Compassion, hear my heartfelt plea,
Grant me the grace to release, to set my spirit free.
For those who have wronged me, I seek a heart unburdened,
Grant me the strength to forgive, to let compassion be awakened.

In the corners of my soul, resentment holds its sway,
But I implore Your mercy, help me find another way.
For in the act of forgiveness, liberation I shall find,
To release the chains of bitterness and nurture a forgiving mind.

Grant me the wisdom to see beyond the pain and strife,
To find compassion in my heart and breathe a new lease of life.
In this evening's stillness, I surrender to Your grace,
Let forgiveness mend my wounded soul, let compassion take its place.

Oh, soothing presence, guide me on this path so steep,
To embrace forgiveness, to let bitterness sleep.
Grant me the strength to let go, to mend what's been torn,
To grant forgiveness, and in turn, be reborn.

As twilight falls and shadows dance, I seek the light within,
To let forgiveness reign, and let healing begin.
In this evening prayer, I offer forgiveness as my plea,
Grant me the grace to forgive, to set my spirit free.

Oh, Divine Love, I surrender to Your guiding hand,
To release the grudges, the resentments, and let forgiveness expand.
In this sacred moment, may forgiveness be my guide,
To embrace compassion, and let resentment subside.

As the night blankets the world, I implore You, hear my cry,
Grant me the strength to forgive, to let resentment die.
May this prayer be heard, and forgiveness bestowed,
That I may heal the wounds, and let compassion unfold.

FORGIVENESS

<u>Prayer 13: Self-Forgiveness</u>

Asking for forgiveness from oneself for mistakes made, shortcomings, or regrets, and embracing self-compassion and healing

In the stillness of this evening, I confront my deepest fears,
I seek forgiveness from within, to dry my river of tears.
For the mistakes I've made, the regrets that haunt my soul,
I plead with myself, grant me forgiveness, to once again feel whole.

Oh, wounded heart, I beg you, release the heavy weight,
For the burdens I carry, let self-forgiveness be my fate.
In this vulnerable moment, I lay my shortcomings bare,
Grant me the grace to forgive myself, to heal and repair.

With a trembling voice, I acknowledge my past mistakes,
The roads I've taken, the wrong turns I did partake.
I yearn for self-compassion, for the scars to slowly mend,
Grant me the strength to forgive myself, to find peace and transcend.

Oh, tormented spirit, hear my plea in this solemn hour,
Grant me the mercy to release the chains of self-blame's power.
In this sacred space, I beseech my own forgiving heart,
To grant me the pardon I seek, a fresh, healing start.

In the twilight's gentle embrace, I confront my inner strife,
Seeking self-forgiveness, to reclaim a precious part of life.
Grant me the courage to face my own reflection with grace,
To forgive myself for mistakes made and let healing take place.

Oh, wounded soul, I beg for your own forgiveness to bestow,
To let go of the past, to allow self-compassion to grow.
In this evening prayer, I implore you to grant me relief,
To embrace self-forgiveness and find solace in self-belief.

As the night unfolds its mysteries, I plead with my own soul,
To grant forgiveness, to nurture a spirit that's whole.
In this moment of reckoning, may self-compassion be my guide,
To forgive myself, let go of regrets, and in love's embrace reside.

Oh, tender presence within, hear my heartfelt plea,
Grant me the strength to forgive myself, to set my spirit free.
In this stillness, let self-forgiveness be the balm that heals,
And may the light of self-compassion illuminate all that conceals.

As twilight fades and darkness claims the sky,
I surrender to self-forgiveness, with a heartfelt sigh.
May this prayer be heard, and self-forgiveness bestowed,
So I may heal my wounded self, and let self-compassion unfold.

FORGIVENESS

Prayer 14: Letting Go

Surrendering the burden of past hurts and resentments, releasing the need for revenge or holding onto grudges, and embracing the freedom that forgiveness brings

In the stillness of this evening, I come to you in prayer,
Seeking the courage to let go, to release burdens I can no longer bear.
For the weight of past hurts and resentments, I plead with all my might,
Grant me the grace to let go, to find freedom in forgiveness' light.

Oh, Divine Guide, hear my humble plea,
Help me surrender the need for revenge, and let forgiveness be.
In this sacred moment, I lay down my grudges and strife,
Grant me the strength to let go, to embrace a renewed life.

With a heavy heart, I carry the weight of past pain,
But I implore you, dear Lord, help me break the chain.
Release me from the clutches of resentment and despair,
Grant me the serenity to let go, to breathe in the healing air.

In the twilight's gentle embrace, I release the need for revenge,
For holding onto grudges only prolongs the pain I avenge.
Grant me the wisdom to see the futility of my strife,
To let go of bitterness and embrace forgiveness in my life.

Oh, Loving Presence, cleanse my wounded soul,
Help me let go of past hurts, to make my spirit whole.
In this solemn hour, I plead for your divine grace,
To release shackles of resentment and find freedom's embrace.

As the night unfolds its mysteries, I humbly surrender,
To let go of past grievances, to let forgiveness render.
Grant me the courage to forgive, to embrace a lighter way,
To let go of the burdens and find peace at the end of the day.

Oh, Divine Light, guide me on this path of release,
To let go of the need for revenge, to find inner peace.
In this evening prayer, I implore you to ease my strife,
Grant me strength to let go and embrace forgiveness in my life.

May this prayer be heard, and my plea be granted,
To let go of past hurts and find the peace I've wanted.
In this sacred surrender, let forgiveness be my guide,
And may I find solace, as I let go and abide.

GUIDANCE

Prayer 15: Divine Guidance

Seeking guidance from a higher power, asking for wisdom
and insight to navigate life's challenges and make decisions
aligned with one's purpose

In the stillness of this evening, I kneel down to pray,
Seeking divine guidance to illuminate my way.
Oh, Higher Power, with humble heart, I earnestly implore,
Grant me your wisdom and insight, forever I'll adore.

In this world of complexities, where choices abound,
I yearn for your guidance, in every step I'm bound.
Illuminate my path, dear Divine, with your radiant light,
So I may tread with certainty, even through the darkest night.

Oh, Heavenly Guide, with each decision I face,
Grant me discernment and clarity, in your infinite grace.
For I am but a vessel, seeking purpose and truth,
In your divine guidance, I find eternal youth.

When doubts and fears creep in, clouding my sight,
I seek your gentle touch, to lead me towards what's right.
Grant me the wisdom to discern, in this intricate dance,
To make choices aligned with my soul's true stance.

As I navigate life's labyrinth, with its twists and turns,
I beseech your guidance, as my spirit yearns.
Pour forth your sacred knowledge, like a soothing stream,
So my decisions may blossom like a fulfilling dream.

Oh, Divine Compass, I surrender to your will,
In your loving presence, my soul finds solace and thrill.
Guide me, dear Higher Power, in each step I take,
Grant me the clarity and insight, for decisions I make.

As the evening draws near, I find solace in this plea,
For your divine guidance, I humbly ask and decree.
In your eternal wisdom, I trust and believe,
That with your loving guidance, I'll triumph and achieve.

GUIDANCE

Prayer 16: Trust and Surrender

Praying for the ability to trust in the unfolding of life and surrendering to divine guidance, letting go of control and seeking guidance in every aspect of life

n the twilight's embrace, I bow my head to pray,
Seeking the strength to trust, to surrender and obey.
Oh, Divine Presence, hear my plea, as I humbly plea,
Grant me the courage to trust, to surrender and be free.

In the ebb and flow of life, uncertainties abound,
I yearn for the grace to trust, to let go, unbound.
Guide me, dear Higher Power, in each step I take,
Grant me the wisdom to surrender, for your sake.

In the depths of my being, I release my grip,
For in surrendering, I find solace, I find the sacred script.
Help me relinquish control, in this uncertain flight,
To trust in your plan, to surrender day and night.

Oh, Divine Guardian, as darkness falls upon the land,
I place my trust in your hands, as I take your loving hand.
In the surrender of my ego, may I find true grace,
And embrace the path you set, at a gentle pace.

In the stillness of this evening, I surrender my fears,
Grant me the serenity to trust, as the path appears.
For in your divine guidance, I find solace and peace,
Help me let go of control, and let divine wisdom increase.

Oh, Sacred Source of love, teach me to trust,
To surrender to your will, to let go of the fuss.
In this prayer of surrender, I find strength anew,
For in trusting and letting go, I find my way to you.

As the stars adorn the sky, and the night grows deep,
I surrender my worries, my burdens, and my sleep.
May your divine guidance lead me to the truth,
In trust and surrender, I find eternal youth.

GUIDANCE

Prayer 17: Inner Wisdom

Asking for the awakening and guidance of one's inner wisdom, tapping into intuition and deep knowing to make choices that align with one's true self

In the twilight's embrace, I seek solace in prayer,
Yearning for inner wisdom, to guide me with care.
Oh, sacred well within me, let your wisdom arise,
Awaken my intuition, beneath these starlit skies.

In the depths of my being, lies a knowing so pure,
A reservoir of wisdom, steady and sure.
Grant me the gift of discernment, dear Divine,
Illuminate my path, with your guidance, divine.

Oh, precious inner wisdom, buried deep within,
I beseech your awakening, as this evening begins.
With a pleading heart, I surrender to your grace,
Guide me on this journey, to find my rightful place.

In the stillness of this hour, I seek your sacred light,
To make choices aligned, with my soul shining bright.
Unveil the answers, hidden in the depths of my soul,
Help me trust in your whispers, to make my life whole.

Oh, gentle inner voice, with your wisdom profound,
Lead me on this path, where true treasures are found.
In the tapestry of life, let me weave with your thread,
As I tap into my intuition, by your wisdom I'm led.

With a humble heart, I plead for your guidance true,
For within me, the answers reside, known only to you.
Illuminate the shadows, reveal the truth within,
Guide me to make choices that align with my kin.

As the night sky unfolds, and the stars shimmer bright,
I seek your inner wisdom, to navigate life's flight.
In the depths of my being, awaken and guide,
Illuminate my path, with your wisdom inside.

Oh, inner wisdom, I surrender to your call,
Guide me on this journey, to stand tall.
In the quiet of this evening, with a heart sincere,
I embrace your whispers and hold your wisdom dear.

GUIDANCE

Prayer 18: Divine Plan

Seeking guidance to understand and align with the greater plan and purpose for one's life, surrendering personal desires and seeking guidance for decisions that serve the highest good

In the depths of the twilight, I bow my head to pray,
Yearning to understand, to walk the destined way.
Oh, Divine Architect, unveil the plan so grand,
Guide me on this journey, with your tender hand.

In the tapestry of life, may I discern my role,
Surrendering my desires, to embrace the greater whole.
Grant me the clarity to see beyond the veil,
To align with the purpose, where love and truth prevail.

Oh, Sacred Weaver, unfold the threads of fate,
Reveal the hidden path, where blessings lie in wait.
In this moment of surrender, I release my will,
Seeking your divine guidance, to fulfill my purpose still.

With a pleading heart, I implore you, dear Divine,
Illuminate the way, where purpose and destiny entwine.
Let my choices be guided by your sacred grace,
To serve the highest good, in every time and place.

As the evening descends, and the stars begin to shine,
May I trust in your plan, with a faith so divine.
In surrendering my desires, I find true liberation,
Aligning with your purpose, in joyful dedication.

Oh, Divine Orchestrator, guide me through the unknown,
Help me embrace the plan, that is uniquely my own.
Grant me the wisdom to discern, with an open heart,
To follow your divine guidance, never to depart.

In the stillness of this evening, I surrender my will,
Seeking your divine plan, to be fulfilled.
Guide me, dear Divine, on this sacred quest,
To live in alignment, where true fulfillment rests.

GUIDANCE

Prayer 19: Openness

Praying for an open mind and heart, willing to receive guidance from unexpected sources, and being receptive to new perspectives

In the stillness of this sacred hour, I kneel and I implore,
Grant me an open heart, dear One, forevermore.
With humility, I seek your grace, an open mind to find,
May my spirit be receptive, as I leave my doubts behind.

I pray for openness, dear Divine, in every breath I take,
To receive your guidance, from any path it may break.
Let not my pride blind me, nor prejudice bind me tight,
Open my soul's eyes, to perceive your guiding light.

In the whispers of the wind, in the silence of the night,
May I hear your gentle voice, guiding me with insight.
Unfold my understanding, as petals of a blooming flower,
So I may embrace the wisdom, descending from your tower.

Grant me the gift of openness, as I journey on my way,
To welcome unfamiliar voices, that cross my path each day.
May my heart be unguarded, free from fear and doubt,
Embracing new perspectives, as I wander all about.

In the embrace of openness, I humbly seek your grace,
To break through the barriers that limit my soul's space.
Guide me to the treasures, hidden in the unknown,
An open heart, an open mind, my spirit fully grown.

With arms outstretched, I pray for openness profound,
To let your love and wisdom in, like whispers without sound.
Guide me, dear Divine, on this wondrous quest,
With openness as my compass, I am eternally blessed.

In this sacred moment, I surrender to your will,
Open my soul, my spirit, let your guidance instill.
May my mind be receptive, my heart forever open,
In the dance of life's mysteries, let your light be woven.

In the twilight's gentle glow, I offer up my plea,
Grant me openness, dear Divine, so I may truly see.
With an open heart and mind, I surrender to your grace,
Leading me on the path of truth, in this sacred space.

STRENGTH

Prayer 20: Resilience

Praying for the strength to bounce back from adversity, to endure hardships, and to find the courage to persevere in the face of challenges

In the depths of weary nights, I come before you, dear Divine,
Seeking strength and resilience, as the challenges intertwine.
Grant me the courage to rise, when the world tries to pull me down,
To face adversity head-on, with a spirit that knows no bounds.

In moments of darkness, when hope seems hard to find,
I plead for resilience, to endure and leave no dreams behind.
When trials come knocking, testing the limits of my soul,
Grant me the strength to stand tall, to overcome and make me whole.

In the face of storms that rage, may my spirit be unyielding,
Grant me resilience, a heart that keeps on healing.
When obstacles block my path, and fear threatens to consume,
Ignite the fire within and grant me strength to bloom.

With every stumble and fall, may resilience be my guide,
To rise up, unbroken, with unwavering stride.
In the crucible of life's challenges, I seek the strength to prevail,
Grant me resilience, dear Divine, when all else seems to fail.

When the weight of the world feels too heavy to bear,
Wrap me in your loving arms, with resilience to share.
Grant me the resilience to weather life's storms,
To face the unknown, with a spirit that transforms.

In this humble prayer, I plead for resilience's embrace,
To navigate the hardships and find solace in your grace.
Grant me the tenacity to persevere, when the journey gets tough,
With resilience as my anchor, I know I'll rise above.

So, I surrender to your divine will, dear Source of Light,
Grant me resilience, to walk through the darkest night.
With every challenge I face, I'll find strength anew,
For in your loving presence, resilience will see me through.

STRENGTH

Prayer 21: Inner Power

Seeking to tap into the wellspring of inner strength,
recognizing and harnessing the power that resides within,
to overcome obstacles and grow stronger

In the depths of twilight's embrace, I humbly come to you,
Yearning for inner power, the strength to see me through.
Grant me, dear Divine, a glimpse of my inner flame,
To rise above the challenges, and never be the same.

Within the depths of my being, a reservoir of might,
I plead for inner power, to guide me through the night.
When darkness clouds my path, and doubts begin to grow,
Illuminate my spirit, and let my inner strength show.

In moments of weakness, when courage starts to wane,
Grant me the inner power, to rise and overcome the pain.
To face the trials that come, with resilience and grace,
And find the strength within, to keep running the race.

Awaken my dormant power, buried deep within my soul,
Grant me the inner strength, to achieve and take control.
In times of uncertainty, when I question my own worth,
Remind me of my power, a force that's bound to surf.

With every breath I take, let my inner power expand,
To face life's battles, with a heart that's brave and grand.
In moments of doubt, when I'm tempted to retreat,
Grant me the inner power, to rise and never admit defeat.

In this sacred prayer, I plead for inner strength so true,
To unlock the power within, that's waiting to breakthrough.
Grant me the wisdom to harness this force so divine,
And let my inner power shine, with a brilliance that's mine.

Oh, source of all power, awaken the fire in my core,
Fill me with inner strength, like never felt before.
With each passing moment, let my power ignite,
To conquer the challenges, and shine with pure light.

So, I surrender to your divine grace, dear Cosmic Guide,
Grant me inner power, as I journey by your side.
In the depths of my being, I seek the strength to flower,
With inner power as my compass, I'll rise and embrace each hour.

STRENGTH

Prayer 22: Guidance and Support

Asking for the strength to seek guidance and support from loved ones, mentors, or a higher power, knowing that strength can be found in community and connection

In the stillness of this evening, I humbly come to pray,
Seeking guidance and support, on this uncertain pathway.
Grant me, dear Divine, the strength to reach out and confide,
In the arms of loving souls, where solace may reside.

When the burdens weigh heavy, and I feel lost and alone,
I plead for guidance and support, to make my heart a home.
Surround me with compassion, from loved ones near and far,
Hold me in your tender embrace, like a guiding star.

In moments of confusion, when choices cloud my mind,
Grant me the strength to seek counsel, from those who are kind.
With their wisdom and insight, may clarity prevail,
Illuminate my path ahead, as I navigate this trail.

Dear mentors and guides, with your wisdom to impart,
I beseech your guidance and support, with an open heart.
Nurture me with your knowledge, and share your precious light,
Help me grow and flourish, as I embrace this sacred fight.

And to the higher power, the source of love and grace,
I plead for guidance and support, to navigate life's maze.
In your divine wisdom, you know my every need,
Guide me on this journey, as my soul continues to feed.

In this tender prayer, I seek strength beyond my own,
To lean on loving hearts, to not face life alone.
Grant me the courage to reach out, to ask for help when needed,
For in unity and connection, true strength is indeed seeded.

So, as the evening unfolds, I offer this plea,
Guide me and support me, in all that I aim to be.
With your loving embrace, I know I can endure,
Thank you for the guidance and support, forever and evermore.

STRENGTH

Prayer 23: Transformation

Praying for the strength to embrace change, to let go of what no longer serves, and to transform challenges into opportunities for growth and personal empowerment

In the hushed whispers of the evening's embrace,
I offer a prayer for transformation and grace.
Grant me strength, dear Divine, to release the old,
And embrace the changes, both gentle and bold.

In the depths of my being, I yearn to grow,
To shed the layers that no longer bestow
The light and the wisdom that I long to find,
Grant me the courage to leave them all behind.

Oh, Great Spirit, guide me through this sacred dance,
As I navigate life's ever-changing expanse.
Help me see the beauty in each turning tide,
And find the strength within, to walk with pride.

Transform my doubts into unwavering belief,
So I may rise above, find solace and relief.
Grant me the vision to see beyond the strife,
And embrace the challenges that shape my life.

With every step forward, I will let go of fear,
For in transformation, a new path will appear.
Grant me the power to face the unknown,
And in its mysteries, may my true self be shown.

In this tender plea, I surrender my will,
To the currents of change, may they shape me still.
Grant me the strength to rise, renewed and whole,
And to embrace transformation, heart, mind, and soul.

As the evening's veil descends, I humbly pray,
For the strength to transform, to walk a new way.
With gratitude in my heart, I surrender, I trust,
That in the journey of transformation, I shall adjust.

So, dear Universe, hear my pleading plea,
Guide me through the fires of transformation's decree.
In your loving grace, I will find my truest form,
And emerge as a soul, reborn and transformed.

STRENGTH

Prayer 24: Courage

Asking for the courage and bravery to confront fears, take
risks, and step outside of one's comfort zone in pursuit of
growth and overcoming obstacles

In the stillness of the evening's gentle sway,
I bow my head and earnestly pray,
Grant me courage, dear Divine, I implore,
To face my fears and open new doors.

Within me lies a strength, yet untapped,
Hidden beneath the shadows, tightly wrapped,
Grant me the bravery to break free,
And embrace the unknown, fearlessly.

In the depths of my heart, doubts reside,
Whispers of worry, relentless and wide,
Grant me the courage to silence their voice,
To make a bold choice, to rise and rejoice.

Oh, Great Spirit, ignite the fire within,
To conquer the battles I must begin,
Grant me the audacity to take a chance,
To dance with uncertainty, in life's intricate dance.

With every step forward, I will shed my doubt,
And embrace the courage that lies without,
Grant me the resilience to face the storms,
To weather the challenges and transform.

In this humble prayer, I humbly ask,
For the courage to complete every task,
To step outside my comfort zone's embrace,
And walk the path that leads to grace.

Grant me the strength to stand tall and strong,
To confront my fears, to right the wrong,
With courage as my guiding light,
I will face the darkness, banish the night.

As the evening's light begins to fade,
I plead for courage, undying and unswayed,
In this sacred hour, I surrender and pray,
For the courage to navigate life's intricate way.

So, dear Universe, hear my plea tonight,
Illuminate my spirit, empower me with might,
Grant me the courage to boldly strive,
To embrace my fears, and truly thrive.

PEACE

Prayer 25: Inner Peace

Praying for a calm and tranquil mind, seeking inner peace
that transcends external circumstances, and finding serenity
amidst life's challenges

In this quiet hour of the eve's embrace,
I bow before you, seeking inner peace's grace,
Grant me, dear universe, a tranquil mind,
That finds solace and serenity, I humbly bind.

Amidst life's chaos and storms that roar,
I beseech you, dear universe, to restore,
The peace within, like a gentle breeze,
That calms my soul, brings me to my knees.

In the depths of turmoil, I long to find,
A sanctuary of peace, a tranquil mind,
Grant me the strength to let go and release,
The burdens that hinder my inner peace.

When worries and anxieties cloud my sight,
I plead for clarity, for peace's guiding light,
May my heart be still, my mind be serene,
In your embrace, dear universe, intervene.

In the midst of noise and discord's strife,
I yearn for harmony, a peaceful life,
Grant me the serenity, like a quiet stream,
To find solace, to find peace in every dream.

When turmoil rages, and storms doth rise,
I pray for inner peace, with tear-filled eyes,
In the depths of my being, may it reside,
As a guiding force, a tranquil tide.

With open palms and a longing soul,
I seek inner peace to make me whole,
Grant me the serenity that transcends,
All external chaos, to which my heart contends.

In this moment of surrender and plea,
I beseech you, dear universe, to set me free,
Grant me the gift of inner peace's grace,
To find solace and serenity in every space.

PEACE

Prayer 26: Peace in Relationships

Praying for harmony and understanding in relationships, seeking to resolve conflicts, and fostering compassion and forgiveness

In the stillness of this evening hour,
I offer a prayer for relationships, dear Power,
Grant us, with pleading hearts, the gift of peace,
In every bond and connection, may strife cease.

In the depths of discord and bitter divide,
I beg for harmony, for wounds to subside,
May understanding bloom where conflict prevails,
And compassion guide our words and tales.

In moments of anger, when tempers flare,
I seek the strength to show kindness and care,
Grant us the wisdom to listen and understand,
To mend what's broken, to heal love's strand.

For those we have hurt, knowingly or unaware,
I plead for forgiveness, a burden we bear,
May hearts soften and resentments dissolve,
As forgiveness and love our spirits evolve.

Let us release judgments and grudges held tight,
Embrace forgiveness, bring darkness to light,
Grant us the grace to rebuild what's been torn,
And create anew a foundation reborn.

In this prayer for peace, may hearts align,
In relationships, may compassion entwine,
May understanding bridge the gaps that divide,
And in unity, love's flame burn bright and wide.

With open palms and humble plea,
I beseech you, dear Power, set us free,
Grant us the harmony and peace we seek,
In relationships, may love's language speak.

As this evening unfolds, may peace descend,
A balm for relationships, a love to mend,
Grant us the grace to foster compassion and care,
In every connection, peace be our shared prayer.

PEACE

Prayer 27: World Peace

Praying for peace and unity among nations, for an end to violence and conflict, and for the well-being and safety of people around the world

In the twilight's embrace, as shadows grow,
I offer a plea for peace to bestow,
Across nations and borders, near and far,
May peace reign supreme, like a guiding star.

With pleading words and a humble heart,
I beseech for unity, a world torn apart,
End the violence, the wars, and strife,
And bring forth an era of harmonious life.

In lands scarred by conflict, where hatred breeds,
I pray for understanding to plant its seeds,
Let compassion rise above the clamor of hate,
And transform divisions into love's open gate.

For those who suffer in the midst of despair,
In war-torn lands, where hope seems rare,
Grant them solace, safety, and relief,
Bring healing to their wounds, mend their grief.

In every corner of this vast earthly sphere,
May all beings find shelter, love, and cheer,
Protect the innocent, the vulnerable, and weak,
And bring an end to the tears they seek.

With open hearts and extended hands,
Let peace bind us all like golden strands,
In unity we stand, one human race,
Together we'll weave a world filled with grace.

So let us pray, in this evening's embrace,
For a world where peace will find its place,
May violence and conflict forever cease,
And the world be adorned with everlasting peace.

PEACE

Prayer 28: Peaceful Coexistence

Praying for tolerance, acceptance, and respect among different cultures, religions, and beliefs, fostering a sense of harmony and coexistence

As twilight descends and stars softly gleam,
I beseech for a world where differences beam,
With pleading words, I lift up my voice,
For peaceful coexistence, let us rejoice.

In a tapestry woven with colors so vast,
May tolerance prevail, erasing the past,
Let acceptance embrace hearts far and near,
Respecting the diversity that makes us appear.

Across cultures and creeds, hand in hand,
May harmony bloom, like a symphony's grand,
For in our differences, strength can be found,
A beautiful mosaic, where unity is crowned.

With open hearts and minds unconfined,
Let love bridge the gaps, leaving biases behind,
In dialogue and understanding, let us engage,
Building bridges of peace with wisdom as our gauge.

No walls shall divide, no hatred shall prevail,
In this prayer for coexistence, we set sail,
May respect guide our actions, gentle and true,
Creating a world where peace steadily grew.

So, let us unite, bound by compassion's embrace,
Embracing diversity with love and grace,
For in the tapestry of humanity we're entwined,
Peaceful coexistence, a prayer intertwined.

PEACE

Prayer 29: Acceptance

Praying for the wisdom and grace to accept things that
cannot be changed, to let go of resistance, and to find
peace in embracing life as it unfolds

As the day draws to a gentle close,
I kneel in prayer, my heart in repose,
With pleading words, I humbly plea,
Grant me the grace of acceptance, I decree.

In the ebb and flow of life's grand design,
Grant me the wisdom to truly align,
To let go of resistance, release the fight,
And find solace in surrendering to what's right.

Grant me the strength to embrace the unknown,
To face the challenges life may have sown,
In every twist and turn, I seek to find,
The peace that comes with an accepting mind.

Help me to see the beauty in each day,
To cherish the moments that come my way,
Let me release the burdens that I bear,
And find serenity in the gifts I share.

Grant me the serenity to accept what's been,
To let go of what cannot be seen,
For in acceptance, I'll find the key,
To unlock the door to inner harmony.

With open arms, I embrace the divine flow,
And in acceptance, my spirit will grow,
For in letting go of resistance's hold,
I'll find peace and blessings to unfold.

In this quiet hour, I humbly implore,
To be granted the grace to accept and adore,
Life's mysteries, its joys and its strife,
And find solace in the acceptance of life.

So, as I close my eyes and release my plea,
May acceptance be the key that sets me free,
In this evening prayer, my heart's desire,
To find peace and serenity that never tires.

HEALING

Prayer 30: Physical Healing

Praying for the restoration of health and well-being for oneself or others who are facing physical ailments, illnesses, or injuries

In the silence of this sacred night,
I offer my prayer, bathed in humble light,
With pleading words, I beseech above,
Grant healing and strength, boundless with love.

For bodies worn by pain and strife,
I pray for healing, the gift of life,
With tender hearts and voices raised,
Let ailments fade and be erased.

Grant solace to those in pain's embrace,
Bring soothing touch and gentle grace,
Restore their bodies, mend what's torn,
Let vibrant health and well-being be reborn.

In this hour of darkness and rest,
I pray for healing, the very best,
May strength surge through veins, revitalized,
And every ache and ailment be exorcised.

Grant doctors wisdom, nurses care,
The healing touch, a gift so rare,
Guide their hands, their minds, their skill,
As they work to restore, to mend, to heal.

For those who suffer, I plead tonight,
May their burdens be eased, their hearts alight,
Renew their spirits, mend their bones,
Let vibrant health in every cell be known.

And for those whose prayers have been unheard,
May hope be kindled, never deferred,
Grant them patience in their time of need,
And the strength to face what lies ahead.

In this evening prayer, my earnest plea,
Let physical healing flow abundantly,
Restore the bodies, mend what's wrong,
And grant the gift of health, resilient and strong.

HEALING

Prayer 31: Emotional Healing:

Requesting healing for emotional wounds, pain, or distress, and praying for comfort, peace, and inner healing for oneself and others who are experiencing emotional turmoil

In the stillness of this twilight hour,
I offer a prayer, my heart's delicate flower,
With pleading words, I humbly beseech,
Grant healing and solace, within our reach.

For hearts burdened by wounds unseen,
I pray for healing, a respite serene,
With tender compassion, I earnestly plead,
Embrace our pain, and sow a new seed.

Grant comfort to those in emotional distress,
Caress their souls, with tenderness,
Wrap them in warmth, and hold them near,
Let healing whispers soothe every tear.

In this hushed moment, as darkness falls,
I pray for emotional healing, within our walls,
May burdens be lifted, sorrows find release,
And hearts be mended, finding inner peace.

Grant strength to face the depths of pain,
With gentle guidance, help us regain,
The lightness of spirit, the joy that's lost,
And heal the wounds, regardless of cost.

For those who carry scars, both old and new,
May healing waters wash away the residue,
Breathe new life into wounded hearts,
And mend the broken pieces, where love departs.

In this evening prayer, I raise my voice,
Seeking emotional healing, a sacred choice,
May burdens be lifted, emotions set free,
And hearts find solace, in sweet harmony.

For those who suffer, in silence they bear,
May healing whispers reach them there,
Wrap them in comfort, like a soothing balm,
And restore their hearts with tranquil calm.

And for myself, I humbly request,
Healing for wounds within my chest,
Grant me the strength to let go and forgive,
And find the courage to truly live.

HEALING

Prayer 32: Spiritual Healing

Seeking spiritual healing and nourishment, praying for a deep sense of connection, inner strength, and a renewed spirit for oneself and others who are seeking spiritual healing

In the twilight's embrace, I humbly pray,
For spiritual healing on this blessed day,
With a pleading heart, I offer my plea,
Grant us solace, oh, Divine Mystery.

In the depths of our souls, where wounds reside,
Pour your healing light, let it gently glide,
Nourish our spirits, restore what's been lost,
In your presence, may we find solace embossed.

For those seeking solace, seeking to find,
A connection profound, a peace of mind,
Wrap them in your love, like a sacred shroud,
Let their spirits soar, above the clouds.

Grant us strength, as we walk this sacred path,
In moments of doubt, shield us from wrath,
Guide our steps, when darkness veils the way,
Illuminate our souls, with your divine ray.

Restore the weary hearts, worn by strife,
Renew our spirits, with abundant life,
Help us transcend, limitations and fears,
And embrace the wisdom that forever endears.

May our spirits be lifted, like birds in flight,
As we seek your presence, in the quiet of night,
Grant us serenity, in times of despair,
And fill our hearts with a love that's rare.

For the seeking souls, yearning to be free,
Grant them solace, as they bow on bended knee,
May they find solace in your eternal embrace,
And feel the warmth of your divine grace.

HEALING

Prayer 33: Mental Healing

Praying for mental clarity, peace of mind, and the healing of mental and psychological challenges, supporting oneself and others who are going through mental health difficulties

In the quiet of this evening's glow,
I offer a prayer, a plea, a gentle flow,
For mental healing, in its tender grace,
A refuge of solace in this sacred space.

With a pleading heart, I seek your light,
To guide me through the darkness of the night,
Grant me clarity, where confusion prevails,
And soothe my mind, as it weaves its tales.

For those burdened by thoughts that weigh them down,
Whose minds wander lost, like a ship unbound,
Wrap them in comfort, with your gentle touch,
Bring tranquility, where chaos feels too much.

Restore their minds, like a calm, still lake,
Where ripples of worry and doubt gently break,
Grant them peace, where storms have waged,
And let their spirits soar, from the cage.

Mend the fractures, the cracks within the mind,
Where anxiety festers, leaving scars behind,
Bring healing balm to wounds unseen,
And unravel the knots where thoughts convene.

May peace settle upon troubled minds,
A sanctuary of calm, where solace finds,
Guide us through the labyrinth of our thoughts,
And untangle the knots, the tangled knots.

Grant us strength to face the battles fought within,
To embrace our minds, flaws and all, let the healing begin,
For mental healing, we humbly implore,
Grant us serenity, forevermore.

In this evening's prayer, we seek your grace,
To mend the fragments of our inner space,
Bring clarity, peace, and a quiet mind,
For mental healing, may we all find.

HEALING

Prayer 34: Collective Healing

Requesting healing for communities, societies, or the world at large, praying for unity, understanding, compassion, and healing from societal issues, conflicts, or divisions

In the twilight's gentle embrace, I kneel and pray,
For collective healing, let our voices convey,
A plea for unity, for hearts to intertwine,
In the depths of our souls, let healing align.

Oh, Divine One, hear this plea so sincere,
For communities wounded, filled with fear,
Unite us, heal us, as one we stand,
Embracing compassion, hand in hand.

Let understanding blossom like a tender flower,
Breaking down walls, with its gentle power,
Heal the divisions that tear us apart,
And mend the wounds that scar each heart.

Guide us, oh, Divine Light, on this sacred quest,
To heal societal issues that burden our chest,
Open our eyes to see the pain others bear,
Ignite in us empathy, love, and care.

Grant us the wisdom to walk the path of peace,
Where differences fade, and unity finds release,
Let healing ripple through every nation,
A balm for the wounds that cause separation.

May compassion flow like a healing stream,
Washing away hatred, as if in a dream,
Rekindle the flame of humanity's heart,
And bridge the divides that keep us apart.

In this evening prayer, I humbly implore,
For collective healing, for wounds to restore,
May love be the salve that binds us tight,
And compassion the guiding star in the night.

May healing extend, beyond our own plight,
To communities, societies, bathed in your light,
Unite us, heal us, as one we become,
In this collective healing, let harmony hum.

Oh, Divine One, let your love be our guide,
As we journey together, side by side,
Grant us the strength to heal and forgive,
And in unity, let our spirits live.

LOVE

Prayer 35: Loving Kindness

Praying for the ability to cultivate a heart of love and kindness, to extend compassion, empathy, and understanding to all beings

In the hush of the evening's embrace,
I come before you, seeking grace,
A plea from my heart, oh Divine above,
Grant me the gift of boundless love.

In this weary world, filled with strife,
I long to embody love in my life,
To cast aside judgment, resentment, and pride,
And let compassion and kindness be my guide.

Oh, Heavenly One, hear my plea,
Open my heart, set my spirit free,
Teach me the ways of love and grace,
To walk in kindness, at a gentle pace.

May love flow from me like a gentle stream,
Touching every soul, like a beautiful dream,
Let me be a vessel of your tender care,
A beacon of love, in a world so unfair.

Grant me the strength to hold another's pain,
To listen with empathy, without disdain,
May my words bring comfort, healing, and peace,
And let my actions make hatred cease.

In every encounter, both big and small,
May love be the language that connects us all,
May I see the beauty in each soul I meet,
And offer compassion, a gift so sweet.

Oh, Divine Source, fill me with love's embrace,
Illuminate my path with your radiant grace,
Guide me to shine love's light so bright,
In every word spoken and every action I ignite.

As the evening descends, I humbly implore,
Help me embody love, forevermore,
May kindness be the legacy I leave behind,
And let love be the essence of my mind.

LOVE

Prayer 36 : Unconditional Love

Praying for the capacity to love others unconditionally,
without expectations or limitations, accepting them for
who they are and showering them with compassion and
kindness

As twilight falls upon this weary day,
I kneel before you, in a humble way,
With a plea for the strength to love, divine,
Unconditionally, with a heart like thine.

Oh, Merciful One, hear my earnest prayer,
Grant me the grace to love, beyond compare,
To embrace others with arms open wide,
In their flaws and virtues, may love reside.

Help me let go of expectations and demand,
To love without limits, to understand,
That love is not bound by conditions or rules,
But a pure essence that transcends and fuels.

In this world of strife and bitter divide,
I beseech thee, grant me love as my guide,
To see beyond the surface, the masks we wear,
And love every soul, with tender care.

Grant me compassion, kind and unending,
For in love's embrace, hearts find mending,
May I be a vessel, a beacon of light,
Shining love's radiance, both day and night.

Teach me to accept others as they are,
With their scars, flaws, and wounds, near and far,
May my love be a shelter, a refuge true,
A sanctuary where they can find love anew.

Oh, Divine Beloved, bestow upon me,
The gift of love, flowing boundlessly,
In every act, every word, every thought,
Let unconditional love be the love I've sought.

LOVE

Prayer 37: Spreading Love

Praying for the opportunity to be a source of love and light in the world, to spread kindness, joy, and compassion to those in need, and to make a positive difference in the lives of others

As the twilight casts its gentle hue,
I kneel before you, my prayer anew.
Oh, hear my plea, my heartfelt desire,
To be a vessel of love, set souls on fire.

Grant me the chance to spread love's embrace,
To touch lives with kindness, leaving a trace.
In a world yearning for hope and relief,
May I be a beacon, a source of belief.

In moments of darkness, anguish, and pain,
May my presence bring solace, like gentle rain.
Let my words be a balm to wounded hearts,
A soothing melody that mends the parts.

Guide my actions, let compassion flow,
In every encounter, let love's light glow.
Help me be a giver of joy and cheer,
To wipe away sorrow, to dry every tear.

In the lives I touch, both near and far,
Let love's radiance be my guiding star.
Through simple acts of kindness and grace,
May I bring smiles to every weary face.

Oh, Divine One, I humbly implore,
Grant me the strength to love even more.
In this broken world, let me be a part,
Of healing and hope, a catalyst for a fresh start.

May my words and deeds be seeds of love,
Sowing compassion, like blessings from above.
In spreading love's warmth, may lives be renewed,
And the world be transformed, one heart at a time.

LOVE

Prayer 38: Healing Relationships

Requesting healing and harmony in relationships, praying for the ability to mend broken connections, foster understanding, and nurture love and compassion within family, friendships, and communities

As the night descends, I kneel and I plea,
For healing in relationships, let it be.
Oh, Divine One, in your mercy and grace,
Mend the broken bonds, let love embrace.

In families torn apart by anger and strife,
Bring reconciliation, restore their life.
Grant them the wisdom to listen and hear,
To let forgiveness replace hurt and fear.

In friendships shattered, wounded and weak,
Ignite understanding, let empathy speak.
May bridges be built, and trust be restored,
In the ashes of discord, let peace be poured.

Within communities, divided and torn,
May unity and harmony be reborn.
Heal the wounds that have caused separation,
And foster love to bridge the separation.

I plead for compassion, both given and received,
To mend the wounds that we've all perceived.
Grant us the strength to choose love over hate,
To nurture connections and break down the gate.

May understanding blossom in every heart,
And forgiveness be the way we all start.
In the healing of relationships, we find,
A love that's resilient, gentle, and kind.

Oh, Divine Healer, hear my humble plea,
Bring healing to relationships, set them free.
May love prevail and harmony reside,
In the bonds we cherish, side by side.

As the evening unfolds, and stars gently gleam,
Let healing flow like a tranquil stream.
In your hands, I place this heartfelt prayer,
For healing relationships, everywhere.

LOVE

Prayer 39: Forgiveness and Compassion

Seeking the strength to forgive others and oneself, and to approach every interaction with compassion, letting go of judgment and embracing a loving perspective

As the sun fades and darkness draws near,
I kneel before you, oh Divine, with a plea sincere,
Grant me the courage to forgive and let go,
To embody compassion, and let kindness flow.

In this world of hurt, anger, and pain,
I yearn for the strength to break the chain,
To release the burden of grudges I hold,
And let forgiveness bloom, like stories of old.

Oh, Heavenly One, hear my humble cry,
Help me embrace the power to reconcile,
May my heart soften, free from resentment's vice,
And see the beauty in others, beyond the disguise.

Grant me the wisdom to understand,
That forgiveness is not weakness, but strength so grand,
Help me release the judgments that bind,
And embrace compassion, with an open mind.

For in forgiveness, true freedom resides,
A healing balm where love and grace abides,
Guide me to forgive, not just others, but me,
To release self-blame and set my spirit free.

Let compassion guide my words and deeds,
A soothing salve for wounds that bleed,
May every interaction be filled with love's touch,
A gentle reminder that we are all human, as such.

In this evening prayer, I plead for the grace,
To forgive, to let go, and to embrace,
Compassion as my guiding light,
To see the world through forgiving sight.

With each passing night, may forgiveness grow,
Bathing my soul in a radiant glow,
And as I seek forgiveness, let me also give,
A tender heart, a compassionate life to live.

In this quiet moment, I humbly pray,
For the strength to forgive, come what may,
May forgiveness and compassion be my creed,
And sow seeds of love, wherever there is need.

PROTECTION

Prayer 40: Divine Protection

Praying for divine protection, asking for guidance, strength, and shelter from any harm or negative influences that may come our way

In the twilight's embrace, I humbly bow,
Seeking refuge from the world's shadows now.
Oh, Divine Protector, hear my plea,
Wrap me in your shelter, set my spirit free.

As I tread the path, unknown and vast,
Guide my steps, let your wisdom hold me fast.
Protect me, dear Guardian, from every harm,
Shield me with your grace, keep me safe and warm.

When troubles arise, like storms that rage,
Be my fortress, my strength in every stage.
Defend me from darkness, negativity's snare,
Surround me with your light, banish every despair.

In moments of weakness, when I falter and sway,
Lend me your courage, help me find my way.
Grant me discernment to navigate life's tide,
And the wisdom to choose, with you as my guide.

Shield my heart from malice, from hatred and strife,
Fill me with compassion, a wellspring of life.
May my words and actions reflect your love,
And radiate kindness, like a gentle dove.

In your embrace, I find solace and peace,
A sanctuary where all worries cease.
Keep me safe, dear Guardian, throughout the night,
And in your loving presence, may I find delight.

With grateful hearts, we lift our voice in prayer,
Seeking divine protection, your tender care.
Oh, Protector Divine, we place our trust in thee,
For in your loving arms, we find sanctuary.

PROTECTION

Prayer 41 : Inner Strength

Seeking inner strength and resilience to face challenges and navigate through difficult situations, allowing us to stay grounded and protected from negative influences

In the depths of my soul, I softly implore,
Grant me inner strength, I seek it once more.
For life's trials and tribulations abound,
I yearn for resilience, to stand my ground.

Oh, source of power that resides within,
Unleash your might, let it now begin.
When storms approach and shadows draw near,
Grant me the courage to overcome fear.

In moments of doubt, when confidence wanes,
Infuse me with strength, like flowing veins.
Help me rise above the challenges I face,
With unwavering spirit, filled with grace.

When chaos surrounds and troubles arise,
Grant me the fortitude to see through the lies.
Protect my heart from negativity's sway,
And guide me towards the brighter way.

In solitude's embrace, I find solace and peace,
A sanctuary where inner strength finds release.
Grant me the wisdom to stay anchored and true,
Shielded from influences that hinder and skew.

With every breath, let resilience ignite,
A flame within me that forever burns bright.
Grant me the strength to endure and prevail,
As I navigate life's winding trail.

Oh, inner strength, I beseech you to rise,
Unleash your power, let it materialize.
In your embrace, I find solace and might,
Guided by your presence, I'll brave the night.

Grant me, dear strength, the gift of resilience,
To face the challenges with unwavering brilliance.
In your sheltering embrace, I humbly reside,
With inner strength as my steadfast guide.

PROTECTION

<u>Prayer 42: Shield of Light</u>

Praying for a protective shield of light to surround us, shielding us from negativity, and allowing only positive energy to enter our lives

In the twilight's hush, I kneel and pray,
Beseeching the heavens in humble display.
Wrap me, oh Divine, in your shield of light,
Protect me from darkness that looms in the night.

With gentle whispers, my plea I impart,
Shield me from shadows that tug at my heart.
Illuminate my path, banish all fear,
Let your radiant glow, in my soul, draw near.

As the stars adorn the vast, velvet sky,
I implore you, dear Universe, hear my cry.
Encircle my being with your radiant grace,
Keep negativity at bay, in every place.

Shield me, oh Light, from the venomous words,
That wound and harm, like sharp-edged swords.
Let kindness and love be my guiding creed,
In your shield of light, I'll find solace indeed.

May your brilliance repel the darkness that seeks,
To dim the light within, with whispers and creaks.
Surround me with your radiance so pure,
A fortress of love that shall endure.

Keep negativity's whispers at bay,
Shield me from their harmful sway.
Let only positivity find its way,
Into my heart, where it may stay.

With each breath, may your light ignite,
A beacon of hope, steadfast and bright.
In your tender embrace, I find reprieve,
From the burdens that weigh, and the shadows that deceive.

Oh, shield of light, hear my fervent plea,
Wrap me in your warmth, set my spirit free.
Guide me on a path of love and compassion,
Shield me from negativity's relentless fashion.

In the stillness of this sacred hour,
I surrender my worries, my fears, my power.
May your divine shield of light always remain,
And in its embrace, may I find peace again.

PROTECTION

Prayer 43: Release of Fear

Requesting the release of fear and anxiety, praying for the courage to overcome fears and to face any potential dangers with a calm and clear mind

In the fading light of day, I come to kneel,
With trembling voice, my fears I reveal.
Oh, sacred Universe, hear my plea,
Grant me the strength to set my fears free.

Release the chains that bind my soul,
From anxious thoughts that take their toll.
With each breath, let courage arise,
To face the shadows, to reach the skies.

When darkness engulfs and doubts descend,
Wrap me in love, a shelter to mend.
Grant me the serenity to let go,
To release the fears that often grow.

May I find solace in your embrace,
As I journey through life's uncertain maze.
Let fear be transformed into bravery's flame,
As I rise above, in your sacred name.

Grant me a calm and clear mind,
To see beyond what fear may find.
May I embrace challenges with open arms,
And find within, the strength that calms.

With each step, guide me through the night,
Illuminate my path with your gentle light.
I plead for the courage to face what's ahead,
To walk through fear, no longer misled.

Oh, Divine Presence, hear my plea,
Grant me the freedom to truly be.
Release the grip of fear's cruel hand,
And guide me to a place of peace, grand.

In the stillness of this evening hour,
I surrender my worries, fears turned sour.
May your love wash over me, and clear,
Any doubts, any worries, any lingering fear.

As the darkness fades and stars ignite,
I trust in your power, your guiding light.
With faith as my shield and love as my guide,
I release fear's hold, with you by my side.

PROTECTION

Prayer 44: Surrounding Loved Ones

Praying for the protection of loved ones, asking for their
safety and well-being, and creating a shield of love and care
around them

As twilight paints the sky in hues of gold,
I kneel before you, my heart unfolds.
Oh, Divine Guardian, hear my plea,
Wrap my loved ones in your arms, set them free.

Protect them, I beg, from harm's cruel touch,
Keep them safe, oh Lord, I love them so much.
Envelop them in a shield of love and care,
Guard their steps, their burdens help them bear.

Wherever they wander, wherever they roam,
Guide them safely, bring them back home.
Shield them from darkness, from troubles and strife,
Bless them with joy, with a purposeful life.

May your light surround them, like a gentle embrace,
Filling their days with love, peace, and grace.
Banish their fears, their worries, their doubt,
Replace them with courage, faith, and clout.

In their laughter and tears, may they find solace,
In their triumphs and trials, may they see your grace.
Grant them strength, oh Lord, in times of despair,
Let them know you're near, that you always care.

Through life's winding journey, be their guiding star,
Illuminate their paths, no matter how far.
Protect them from harm, both seen and unseen,
In your sheltering love, may they always glean.

Oh, Divine Protector, heed my plea,
Surround my loved ones, keep them close to thee.
With gratitude in my heart, I offer this prayer,
For their safety and well-being, in your loving care.

REFLECTION

Prayer 45: Self-Awareness

Praying for increased self-awareness, seeking clarity and understanding of one's thoughts, emotions, and actions, and embracing personal growth through introspection

In the twilight's embrace, I humbly bow,
Seeking self-awareness, dear Guide, allow.
Grant me the wisdom to look within,
To explore my thoughts, where they begin.

In the depths of my heart, may I find,
A mirror to reflect my inner mind.
Illuminate the corners I can't see,
Reveal the truths that lie deep within me.

Guide me through the labyrinth of my soul,
Uncover the patterns that take their toll.
May I understand my emotions' sway,
And navigate life with greater insight each day.

Grant me the courage to face my flaws,
To embrace the shadows and their cause.
For in self-awareness, I find the key,
To unlock the doors that set me free.

With each step I take, may clarity grow,
In thoughts, words, and actions, may it show.
Grant me the strength to change what I must,
To transform my weaknesses into trust.

I plead for your guidance on this journey I'm on,
To know myself deeply, and to become strong.
In self-awareness, I'll find the way,
To grow, to evolve, and to seize each new day.

As evening descends and darkness falls,
I turn to you, dear Guide, with pleading calls.
Grant me the gift of self-awareness divine,
So I may walk this path with purpose and shine.

REFLECTION

<u>Prayer 46: Letting Go</u>

Reflecting on any negative emotions, regrets, or attachments accumulated throughout the day, and praying for the strength and willingness to let go, allowing space for growth and healing

As the night draws near, I bow my head,
Seeking solace in the words left unsaid.
In this sacred moment, I humbly plea,
Grant me the strength to set my burdens free.

Release the weight that weighs upon my heart,
The regrets, the sorrows tearing me apart.
With trembling hands, I offer up my pain,
And surrender to the healing, like gentle rain.

For in letting go, I find my release,
A balm for the soul, a newfound peace.
I beg for your guidance on this sacred night,
To loosen my grip and let go with all my might.

Help me release attachments that hold me tight,
And find the courage to embrace the light.
Let me release the wounds that pierce my soul,
And find the strength to make myself whole.

With each breath, I surrender and let be,
The fears, the worries, no longer controlling me.
Grant me the wisdom to forgive and forget,
To move forward with a heart that's no longer beset.

In the stillness of this evening's grace,
I surrender, I let go, and find my place.
With open hands, I release what's been,
And welcome the healing that will begin.

As I close my eyes and lay my burdens down,
May I find solace in the peace I have found.
In this moment of surrender and release,
Grant me the serenity and inner peace.

REFLECTION

Prayer 47: Setting Intentions

Engaging in reflection to set positive intentions for personal growth, envisioning the person one aspires to become, and seeking guidance to align actions and thoughts accordingly

In the twilight's gentle embrace,
I offer my soul, seeking solace and grace.
With humble heart and fervent plea,
I yearn for guidance to set intentions free.

In the depths of self-reflection's gaze,
I seek the path where true growth plays.
Grant me the wisdom to envision anew,
The person I aspire to be, honest and true.

Guide me, O Divine, in this sacred quest,
To align my actions with intentions blessed.
May my thoughts be pure, my heart be kind,
As I navigate the labyrinth of the mind.

Grant me the strength to let go of the old,
To release the patterns that no longer hold.
With each breath, may clarity arise,
As intentions manifest before my eyes.

In the stillness of this prayerful hour,
Fill my spirit with purpose and power.
With open arms, I surrender my will,
May my intentions bloom and fulfill.

For in setting intentions, I sow the seed,
To create a life aligned with my soul's creed.
May my words and deeds reflect the light,
As I journey towards my highest height.

In this twilight hour, I make my plea,
To set intentions that will set me free.
Guide me, dear Universe, in this sacred dance,
As I embrace the power of intention's chance.

REFLECTION

Prayer 48: Embracing Change

Reflecting on areas of life that require change or improvement, and praying for the courage, motivation, and resilience to embrace change, step out of comfort zones, and strive for personal growth

As the evening's gentle whispers descend,
I come before you, my heart on the mend.
In the depths of my soul, I humbly confess,
The need for change, the longing to progress.

Grant me, O Divine, the courage to let go,
Of the familiar paths I've come to know.
For growth lies beyond comfort's embrace,
In the realm of change, where new horizons grace.

I plead for motivation to ignite my flame,
To rise above complacency, to never be the same.
Grant me the strength to face my fears,
To venture into the unknown, despite the tears.

In the quiet of this sacred hour,
May resilience bloom and empower.
Guide my steps as I embrace the unknown,
With each stride, may my spirit be grown.

Open my eyes to the lessons that await,
In the twists and turns, in the choices I make.
Let change be my ally, my catalyst for light,
As I embark on this transformative flight.

Grant me the wisdom to discern the way,
To navigate the currents, to seize the day.
In the face of uncertainty, let faith abide,
As I surrender to change, with arms open wide.

In this evening's prayer, I humbly seek,
The courage to change, the strength to peak.
Embrace my plea, O Universe divine,
Guide me on this journey of change, as it intertwines.

REFLECTION

Prayer 49: Seeking Inner Guidance

Requesting clarity and insight during moments of reflection, asking for guidance to understand oneself better and make positive choices for personal growth

In the stillness of this evening's embrace,
I come before you with a heart full of grace.
With humble words, I seek your inner light,
To guide me through the shadows of the night.

Grant me, O Divine, a spark of your wisdom,
In moments of reflection, when doubts may come.
With pleading heart, I ask for clarity's hand,
To understand myself, to truly understand.

In the depths of my soul, there's a yearning desire,
To unravel the mysteries that often transpire.
I seek your guidance, a compass to lead,
Through the labyrinth of thoughts that I need.

Illuminate my path with your gentle insight,
Help me discern between wrong and right.
In the tapestry of choices, let me see,
The threads of my purpose, my destiny.

Grant me the courage to listen within,
To the whispers of truth, where answers begin.
In this sacred space of self-discovery,
May your presence be felt, guiding me gently.

With each step I take, may clarity arise,
And unveil the path that leads to the skies.
In moments of reflection, may I find,
The wisdom I need, the peace of mind.

As the evening's veil descends upon the land,
I seek your guidance, O Divine hand.
Guide me, enlighten me, in the choices I make,
In seeking inner truth, for my spirit's sake.

UNITY

Prayer 50: Global Harmony

Praying for unity and harmony among all nations and cultures, asking for the dissolution of barriers and prejudices, and envisioning a world where diversity is celebrated and respected

In the stillness of this evening's embrace,
I bow my head and seek your grace.
A plea from the depths of my weary soul,
For global harmony to make us whole.

O Merciful One, hear my prayer,
May unity and peace be our shared affair.
Break down the walls that divide our hearts,
Let love and understanding be the start.

In a world plagued by prejudice and strife,
I long for a tapestry woven with threads of life.
A tapestry where colors blend in harmony,
Celebrating diversity, a symphony.

Oh, let our differences be bridges, not walls,
Where understanding triumphs and compassion calls.
May respect replace hatred's bitter seed,
And prejudice vanish, never again to feed.

Let kindness be the language we all speak,
Embracing each other, the strong and the weak.
For in unity lies our true strength and power,
To build a world where harmony flowers.

I plead with you, O Divine Source,
Guide us towards a future, a new course.
Where nations join hands in a dance of peace,
And global harmony, our souls release.

May this prayer touch the hearts of all,
From every corner of the world, great and small.
In this evening's stillness, let hope arise,
A world united under your loving skies.

UNITY

Prayer 51: Inner Unity

Seeking inner unity and peace within oneself, praying for the integration of mind, body, and spirit, and cultivating a sense of wholeness and harmony in personal thoughts and actions

In the depths of this tranquil eve,
A plea emerges, my soul believes.
Grant me, O Divine, a sacred space,
Where inner unity finds its embrace.

I yearn for harmony within my core,
Where mind, body, and spirit restore.
Align my thoughts with wisdom's light,
To banish chaos and find respite.

With humble words, I make my plea,
Merge the fragments inside of me.
Fuse my mind, body, and spirit true,
In perfect union, like morning dew.

Grant me the strength to let go of strife,
And welcome peace into my life.
May serenity bloom in every breath,
As I journey toward inner wholeness.

O Divine One, hear this humble cry,
Grant me the wings of unity to fly.
Unite the fragmented pieces within,
So I may know the grace of peace again.

In this evening's stillness, I implore,
Guide me to the path of inner shore.
Where unity reigns and discord flees,
And I find solace within, at ease.

UNITY

Prayer 52: Healing Divisions

Praying for the healing of divisions and conflicts within communities and societies, asking for compassion, understanding, and the willingness to bridge differences in the pursuit of unity

In the hush of this sacred night,
I kneel before you, my plea in sight.
Grant me strength, O gracious divine,
To heal the divisions that intertwine.

In a world torn by conflicts deep,
Where unity seems but a distant leap,
I pray for compassion to light the way,
To mend the divisions that cloud our day.

With humbled heart, I ask for grace,
To see beyond our differences' embrace,
To foster understanding, let judgment cease,
And find the common thread that brings us peace.

Grant us the wisdom to bridge the divide,
To stand united, hand in hand, side by side,
May empathy guide each word we speak,
And empathy heal the wounds that run deep.

O Divine One, with an earnest plea,
I ask for unity, for harmony to be.
Heal the divisions that tear us apart,
And ignite love's flame within each heart.

As the stars twinkle above in the sky,
May divisions dissolve, grievances fly,
And in their place, let unity reside,
A tapestry woven with threads of compassion, side by side.

Grant us the courage to seek common ground,
To celebrate our differences, joyfully profound,
In healing divisions, we find the way,
To build a world united, every single day.

UNITY

Prayer 53: Empathy and Connection

Requesting the ability to empathize with others, to recognize our shared humanity, and to cultivate meaningful connections that foster unity and mutual respect

In this quiet hour, I humbly pray,
For empathy to light my way.
Grant me the gift to truly see,
The world through eyes that aren't just me.

Oh, Divine Source, I long to feel,
The pain and joy that others conceal.
Break down the walls that keep us apart,
Ignite a fire within my heart.

Grant me the grace to understand,
The struggles faced in every land.
May I embrace our shared connection,
And foster unity through deep reflection.

In moments when division's strong,
May empathy guide me all day long.
To walk beside my fellow soul,
And let compassion make us whole.

Help me build bridges, tear down walls,
To hear the silent cries and calls.
May I be a vessel of love and care,
A beacon of hope in a world so unfair.

Through empathy, may I extend my hand,
To all who need a friend to understand.
In fostering connections, may we find,
A unity that transcends space and time.

So, I plead with all my heart and soul,
Grant me the gift to make empathy my goal.
To see the beauty in our diversity,
And nurture a world filled with unity.

UNITY

Prayer 54: Oneness with Nature

Praying for a deeper connection with the natural world, recognizing that we are part of a greater whole, and seeking unity and harmony with the Earth and all living beings

In this twilight's hush, I bow my head,
To nature's wisdom, I humbly tread.
Oh, gentle Earth, your beauty I adore,
Please grant me oneness, forevermore.

With each passing breeze, I long to feel,
The sacred secrets that you conceal.
Oh, whisper to me in melodies untold,
And let my spirit merge with yours, behold.

In the rustling leaves and flowing streams,
In sunlight's warmth and moonlit dreams,
I seek a connection, deep and true,
To be one with nature, as I yearn to do.

Grant me the grace to hear your call,
In every creature, both big and small.
Help me see the divine in every tree,
And cherish the gift of this unity.

Let me walk gently upon your ground,
With reverence and love that knows no bound.
For we are but guests in your sacred space,
Oh, Earth, may we honor your divine grace.

In your embrace, may I find solace and peace,
A symphony of life that will never cease.
May my actions align with your sacred dance,
And together, we'll create a harmonious trance.

So, I plead with all my heart and soul,
To be one with nature, to make it whole.
Grant me the wisdom to cherish and preserve,
This precious connection, for which I fervently serve.

HOPE

Prayer 55: Light in Darkness

Praying for the presence of hope and light during times of
darkness and despair, seeking solace and strength to
overcome challenges and find renewed optimism

In the depths of night, I raise my plea,
A prayer for light when darkness envelops me.
Oh, bring forth hope to illuminate my way,
And guide me through the shadows day by day.

When despair descends like a heavy shroud,
And doubt and fear try to hold me bound,
I beg for a glimmer, a flicker of light,
To pierce through the darkness, shining so bright.

Grant me the strength to face each trial,
To find resilience when life seems vile.
With every challenge, let courage arise,
And let hope be the spark that never dies.

In the darkest moments, when all seems lost,
I implore for a beacon, no matter the cost.
For in the face of adversity, I'll prevail,
With the light of hope, I shall never fail.

May it lead me to paths unknown and new,
Where dreams take flight and possibilities accrue.
So, I beseech you, oh divine and wise,
Infuse my spirit with hope that never dies.

With humble heart, I offer this prayer,
To find solace in darkness, for light to be there.
In the face of despair, may hope ignite,
And guide me towards a future so bright.

HOPE

Prayer 56: Renewed Faith

Requesting the restoration of faith and trust in the journey of life, praying for the belief that better days lie ahead and that challenges can be transformed into opportunities

In the quiet of this evening's embrace,
I come before you, seeking solace and grace.
With a pleading heart, I humbly pray,
For a renewed faith to light my way.

When doubts and shadows cloud my mind,
And hope seems distant, so hard to find,
Restore my trust in the path I tread,
Renew my faith in the words you've said.

Grant me the strength to face each test,
To rise above and give my very best.
For in every challenge, a seed may grow,
An opportunity for my spirit to glow.

When darkness looms and doubts persist,
Help me see the lessons within the mist.
Guide me to embrace life's ebb and flow,
With renewed faith, I'll surely grow.

Let each setback be a stepping stone,
To a brighter future, yet unknown.
In the face of trials, grant me the sight,
To see the blessings hidden in plain sight.

So, I beseech you, with all that I am,
Restore my faith like a flickering flame.
Let it burn strong, unwavering and true,
As I trust in the journey, guided by you.

May my heart be filled with hope's sweet song,
As I navigate this path, however long.
With renewed faith, I'll embrace each day,
Knowing better times are on their way.

HOPE

Prayer 57: Inner Resilience/Transformation

Praying for the resilience and courage to face adversity with hope, seeking the strength to persevere and find new possibilities even in the midst of difficult circumstances

In the depths of this evening's hour,
I come to you with a plea, O Power.
Grant me strength, unwavering and true,
To face life's trials, and emerge anew.

When darkness falls and shadows creep,
When the world feels heavy, and troubles seep,
Instill in me a resilient heart,
To navigate storms, and never fall apart.

In the face of adversity, I seek your grace,
To rise above challenges and find my place.
Grant me courage to confront what's unknown,
To transform setbacks into seeds I've sown.

When the road is steep and obstacles loom,
Help me persevere, dispelling all gloom.
Guide me to find silver linings within,
And discover new possibilities to begin.

May I be like the phoenix, rising from ash,
Transforming struggles into growth in a flash.
Grant me the wisdom to learn from each test,
And find resilience in my very best.

In times of despair, let hope be my guide,
As I navigate life's twists and abide.
With a pleading heart, I seek your aid,
To transform challenges into steps forward laid.

Grant me resilience to weather life's storm,
To find inner strength, even when forlorn.
In this evening prayer, I humbly implore,
The power to transform and emerge even more.

HOPE

Prayer 58: Inspiring Vision

Seeking a vision of hope that inspires and motivates,
praying for clarity and insight to envision a brighter future
and the determination to work towards it

In the hushed whispers of the twilight hour,
I kneel before you, yearning for your power.
Grant me, dear Creator, a vision divine,
To ignite my spirit and make it shine.

In the depths of my soul, I plead for sight,
A vision of hope to guide me through the night.
Oh, grant me clarity to see beyond the veil,
A glimpse of the future where dreams prevail.

Illuminate my path with a radiant light,
So I may soar beyond my current plight.
Fill my heart with inspiration's fire,
Igniting within me an unwavering desire.

Grant me a vision that's bold and true,
A beacon of hope that will see me through.
For in this prayer, I seek the strength and will,
To shape a future where dreams fulfill.

With determination, I'll tread the unknown,
With unwavering faith, my purpose will be shown.
Let me see the beauty of what lies ahead,
And with each step, may my vision be spread.

In this evening's plea, I humbly implore,
A vision of hope that my spirit may soar.
Grant me the clarity, dear Lord above,
To envision a future filled with boundless love.

HOPE

Prayer 59: Collective Hope

Praying for hope to extend beyond oneself, seeking hope for others who may be struggling, and fostering a sense of unity and support to uplift one another in times of despair

In the quiet of this evening's embrace,
I bow my head, seeking solace and grace.
With a humble plea, I lift my voice high,
Praying for collective hope that reaches the sky.

Oh, dear Divine, hear my heartfelt plea,
Let hope flow like a river, wide and free.
Extend it beyond myself, far and near,
To those in darkness, let its light appear.

I beseech you, Creator, in this hour of need,
For those who are weary, let hope take the lead.
Wrap them in your love, like a gentle embrace,
Fill their hearts with courage, strength, and grace.

May hope's radiant flame, fierce and bright,
Guide us through the darkest of nights.
Unite us as one, in a tapestry of care,
So no one feels alone, burdened, or despair.

Let us lift each other, hand in hand,
Building bridges of hope across the land.
In our collective hope, may we find,
Strength, resilience, and peace of mind.

Grant us the power to inspire, to uplift,
To be a beacon of hope, a soothing gift.
For in unity, dear Lord, we shall find,
A world where hope prevails, infinitely kind.

So, on this eve, I humbly implore,
Fill our hearts with hope, forevermore.
Let it bind us together, in a tapestry divine,
A symphony of hope, in this prayer of mine.

FAITH

<u>Prayer 60: Guidance and Wisdom</u>

Praying for guidance and wisdom from a higher power, seeking clarity and understanding in one's faith journey, and trusting in divine guidance

In the quiet of this evening's embrace,
I humbly kneel, seeking your loving grace.
With trembling words, I raise my plea,
Guide me, oh Higher Power, set my spirit free.

In the depths of my soul, I yearn for your light,
A beacon of wisdom, shining ever so bright.
Grant me the knowledge, the understanding profound,
To navigate this journey, where answers are found.

Oh, Divine Source, I beg for your hand,
Lead me through life's maze, help me understand.
In moments of doubt, when shadows appear,
Illuminate my path, make your presence clear.

Grant me the discernment to know right from wrong,
To hear your whispers amidst the chaotic throng.
With every step I take, let your wisdom be my guide,
So I may walk in faith, with you by my side.

Pour your wisdom into my heart and mind,
Let it flow through me, pure and unconfined.
Help me decipher life's intricate design,
And find solace in the answers I shall find.

In this humble prayer, I place my trust,
Knowing that you hear me, dear Lord, you must.
Guide me along the path that's meant for me,
With your divine guidance, my spirit shall be free.

FAITH

Prayer 61: Surrender and Trust

Requesting the ability to surrender worries, fears, and uncertainties to a higher power, trusting that everything is in divine hands and that there is a greater plan at work

In this hushed moment of twilight's embrace,
I humbly kneel, seeking your comforting grace.
With a pleading heart, I offer my plea,
Help me surrender, dear Lord, and trust in thee.

Release the worries that burden my soul,
The fears that consume, the doubts that take their toll.
In this surrender, I find solace and rest,
Trusting that you, dear God, know what is best.

For in your hands, the universe unfolds,
A grand design, more intricate than can be told.
Though uncertainties dance like shadows in my mind,
I surrender them all, leaving them behind.

With open palms, I let go of control,
Embracing the peace that comes from surrender's toll.
For I know, dear Lord, you hold the master plan,
And in your loving care, I firmly stand.

Guide me, oh Divine, with your gentle touch,
Whispering wisdom that means so much.
Help me trust in the path that lies ahead,
Knowing that by your grace, I will be led.

In this evening's prayer, I offer my plea,
Surrendering my worries, placing my trust in thee.
May I find comfort in surrender's embrace,
And through trust in you, find abundant grace.

FAITH

Prayer 62: Deepening Connection

Seeking a deeper connection with a higher power, praying
for a stronger relationship and communion, and nurturing a
sense of closeness and trust

In the stillness of this evening's embrace,
I humbly kneel, seeking your sacred grace.
With pleading words, I lay my heart bare,
Yearning for a connection, a divine affair.

Oh, Higher Power, hear my heartfelt plea,
Grant me the gift of deepening intimacy.
In this vast universe, so vast and wide,
I long to feel your presence by my side.

Wrap me in your love, like a gentle embrace,
Guide me through darkness, with your radiant grace.
Deepen the bond we share, in sacred communion,
Fill my soul with awe and divine union.

In the quiet moments, as I seek your face,
Draw me closer to you, in your infinite space.
Illuminate my path, with your guiding light,
And let me bask in your wisdom and insight.

May our connection grow stronger each day,
As I walk in faith, and in your presence stay.
Nurture this bond, with your divine touch,
For in your embrace, I find solace so much.

In this evening prayer, I humbly implore,
A deeper connection, forevermore.
May my heart be open, receptive, and true,
As I journey closer, dear Lord, to you.

FAITH

Prayer 63: Gratitude for Divine Presence

Expressing gratitude for the constant presence and support
of a higher power in one's life, recognizing the blessings
and guidance received along the journey

In the twilight's gentle glow, I humbly kneel,
With a heart full of gratitude, I deeply feel.
Oh, Divine Presence, with love and awe I pray,
For your unwavering guidance, each and every day.

In the depths of my soul, I sense your embrace,
A comforting presence, a tender grace.
Through trials and triumphs, you've been my guide,
In moments of darkness, you've stood by my side.

With a pleading tone, I express my deep gratitude,
For the blessings bestowed, in magnitude.
Your wisdom and love, a divine symphony,
Guiding my steps, in this earthly journey.

For the lessons learned, both joyous and tough,
For the strength you provide when the road gets rough,
For the gentle whispers that light my way,
I offer my thanks, in humble words I say.

In the tapestry of life, your hand I see,
Weaving miracles and blessings, setting me free.
Your presence, a constant source of hope and light,
Guiding me forward, in your loving sight.

So tonight, dear Lord, as I end this day,
I offer my gratitude in a heartfelt way.
May my words reach you, like a gentle breeze,
And may my thanks bring you joy and ease.

For your unwavering presence, I am forever blessed,
In your divine embrace, I find solace and rest.
With profound gratitude, I humbly confess,
My life is enriched by your love and tenderness.

FAITH

Prayer 64: Strengthening Faith in Times of Doubt

Praying for strength and resilience in moments of doubt or
spiritual struggles, asking for the ability to trust and believe,
even when faced with uncertainty

In the depths of the night, I kneel and plea,
A soul lost in doubts, seeking clarity.
Oh, Higher Power, in this moment of strife,
Grant me the strength to embrace a steadfast life.

When shadows cast doubt upon my weary soul,
When questions arise, threatening to take control,
I humbly implore you, dear Divine,
Guide me through this darkness, let your light shine.

In the face of uncertainty, my faith may waver,
Yet deep within, a flicker of hope I endeavor.
Grant me resilience to withstand the test,
To find solace and peace in the midst of unrest.

When doubts cloud my vision, like a veil so dense,
Ignite the fire of belief, dispel the suspense.
Wrap me in your embrace, with love so true,
Renew my faith, let it bloom and accrue.

In moments of weakness, when doubts abound,
Fill me with courage, let inner strength resound.
For I long to trust, to believe in your plan,
To walk with conviction, guided by your hand.

Grant me the patience to endure this trial,
To find solace in faith, mile after mile.
In my pleading, may I find solace and peace,
And from doubts and uncertainty, may I release.

Oh, Higher Power, as I pour out my heart,
Grant me the fortitude to make a fresh start.
Strengthen my faith in times of doubt and dismay,
For in your loving presence, doubts shall fade away.

COMPASSION

Prayer 65: Cultivating a Loving Heart

Praying for the ability to cultivate a heart filled with compassion, kindness, and love towards oneself and others

In the stillness of this evening's embrace,
I humbly come to you, seeking your grace.
Oh, Higher Power, hear my fervent plea,
Grant me a heart that loves unconditionally.

In a world filled with strife and disdain,
May my heart be a beacon of love's domain.
With every beat, let compassion flow,
And kindness blossom wherever I go.

Grant me the strength to forgive and mend,
To embrace others as my dear friend.
In moments of anger, let love prevail,
And may empathy and understanding never fail.

Oh, Divine Source, with utmost humility,
I ask for the gift of a loving heart's ability.
Teach me to cherish, to uplift, and to serve,
To find joy in giving, with no expectation in return.

Let me see the beauty in every soul I meet,
To offer a smile, a comforting retreat.
May my words be gentle, my actions kind,
In this world, may love be the tie that binds.

As I cultivate a loving heart within,
May it radiate without, touching hearts akin.
Grant me the grace to heal, to console,
To be a vessel of love, making a difference, whole.

In this prayer, I surrender my plea,
To become an instrument of love, so free.
Oh, Higher Power, bless me with this art,
To cultivate a loving heart, in every part.

COMPASSION

Prayer 66: Empathy for Others

Seeking the capacity to understand and empathize with the experiences, emotions, and struggles of others, praying for the ability to walk in their shoes and offer support

In the stillness of this evening's embrace,
I come to you, seeking your boundless grace.
Grant me, dear Higher Power, the gift to see,
The world through eyes of empathy.

In a world that often feels so cold,
I yearn for a heart that's gentle and bold.
Oh, let me feel what others feel,
Their joys and sorrows, so raw and real.

Open my eyes to the struggles they face,
Grant me the wisdom to hold their space.
In their shoes, let me humbly walk,
With compassion and kindness as my talk.

Give me the patience to truly listen,
To understand their pain, without condition.
May I offer solace when tears run deep,
A shoulder to lean on, a soul to keep.

Help me set aside my judgments and pride,
To see the humanity we all hide.
For in our shared experiences, we find,
A bond that can heal, unite, and bind.

I plead for the strength to offer support,
To lend a helping hand, a comforting sort.
May my presence bring solace and peace,
A sanctuary where their troubles can cease.

Dear Higher Power, hear my earnest plea,
Grant me the empathy that sets others free.
In this prayer, my heart is alight,
With the desire to love, to understand, and unite.

COMPASSION

<u>Prayer 67: Compassion in Action</u>

Requesting guidance and strength to actively demonstrate compassion through acts of kindness, generosity, and service to those in need

In this twilight's gentle glow,
I bow my head, my spirit low.
With a plea that echoes deep within,
Grant me the grace to let compassion begin.

Oh, Higher Power, source of light,
Guide my steps through the darkest night.
Grant me strength and wisdom to embrace,
The power of compassion in every place.

In a world burdened by pain and strife,
Let me be the beacon, the source of life.
Ignite in me a fire, burning bright,
To serve others with love and selfless might.

Grant me the eyes to see the unseen,
The broken hearts and dreams unseen.
May my hands be open, ready to give,
To those in need, so they may live.

With each act of kindness, let love flow,
A balm to heal wounds, to help them grow.
Let me be the vessel of your grace,
Spreading compassion in every space.

Teach me to listen, to lend an ear,
To wipe away every sorrowful tear.
May my actions speak louder than words,
A testament to compassion that soars.

For in serving others, we find our worth,
A purpose that transcends this earthly birth.
So I implore you, in this humble prayer,
Grant me compassion in actions I share.

In your hands, I place my plea,
To be a vessel of love and unity.
With your guidance, I will faithfully strive,
To bring compassion alive.

COMPASSION

Prayer 68: Forgiveness and Understanding

Praying for the grace to forgive others and oneself,
embracing a compassionate perspective that recognizes the
shared humanity and fallibility of all beings

In the stillness of this twilight hour,
I humbly come before your power.
With a plea that weighs upon my soul,
Grant me the grace to forgive and make whole.

Oh, Divine Presence, hear my plea,
Unburden my heart and set me free.
Grant me the strength to let go of the past,
To release resentment that holds me fast.

For in the depths of forgiveness lies,
A liberation that helps us rise.
To understand the frailties we share,
And embrace compassion beyond compare.

Grant me the wisdom to see with new eyes,
The struggles and pain that others disguise.
May empathy guide my every thought,
A balm of understanding, dearly sought.

Let me extend compassion's hand,
To heal wounds that time cannot withstand.
For in forgiveness, we find release,
A path to harmony and inner peace.

And as I seek forgiveness for my own mistakes,
Grant me the grace to learn from each heartache.
To embrace my imperfections with gentle care,
And find the strength to rise and repair.

In this prayer, I ask for your divine grace,
To heal the wounds that time cannot erase.
May forgiveness mend what's been torn asunder,
And help us find unity and love, as we ponder.

For in forgiveness, we discover the way,
To let go of resentment that colors our day.
Grant me the courage to forgive, I implore,
And let understanding and love restore.

COMPASSION

Prayer 69: Acts of Kindness

Requesting opportunities to engage in acts of kindness and compassion, praying for the awareness and willingness to extend a helping hand and make a positive difference in the lives of others

In the quiet of this evening's embrace,
I kneel before you, seeking your grace.
Grant me the chance, dear divine above,
To sow seeds of kindness and spread love.

With pleading heart and humble plea,
Open my eyes so I may truly see,
The ones in need, the burdened and lost,
Grant me the awareness, no matter the cost.

In a world that often turns a blind eye,
Let me be the beacon, the reason why,
I extend my hand to those in despair,
To show them that someone truly does care.

Grant me the strength to make a difference,
To offer solace, kindness, and assistance.
In acts both grand and small, let me partake,
A vessel of love, with no act too small to undertake.

May I bring comfort to the broken and weary,
To the lonely souls, downtrodden and teary.
With empathy as my guiding light,
May I ease their burdens, bring them respite.

In this evening prayer, I humbly implore,
To be an instrument of kindness, forevermore.
Grant me the opportunities, both seen and unseen,
To brighten lives, to fulfill a purpose serene.

For it's through acts of compassion we find,
The true essence of life, the purpose enshrined.
So, I beseech you, dear divine, I pray,
Let me be a vessel of kindness each day.

LETTING GO

Prayer 70: Detachment

Praying for the strength to detach from outcomes, possessions, and relationships, surrendering the need for control and embracing the flow of life as guided by a higher power

In the stillness of this evening's plea,
I come before you, with a heart set free.
Grant me the strength, dear divine above,
To detach from what I cannot truly love.

With pleading words and a humble prayer,
Release me from attachments, let me dare,
To let go of outcomes, possessions, and more,
And surrender to the flow, as I've done before.

In a world that craves control and clings tight,
Grant me the courage to release my might,
To loosen the grip on what I hold so dear,
And trust in your guidance, void of fear.

Detach me from the need to always know,
To pave my path, and have the final say so.
For in surrender lies a deeper grace,
A freedom from burdens that I embrace.

Help me detach from relationships that bind,
Where expectations cloud the heart and mind,
Grant me the wisdom to let go with grace,
To allow space for growth and a sacred space.

In this evening's prayer, I humbly beseech,
To detach from what weighs me down, out of reach.
Grant me the serenity to release my control,
And trust in your plan, to make me whole.

For it's in detachment, I find liberation,
A surrender that leads to transformation.
So, I implore you, dear divine, I pray,
Grant me the strength to detach each day.

LETTING GO

Prayer 71: Trust in Divine Timing

Seeking the ability to trust in the perfect timing of events, praying for the patience and understanding to let go of the need for immediate results and to surrender to the divine timing of the universe

In this evening's quiet embrace,
I humbly come before your grace,
I pray for trust, with heartfelt plea,
In the divine timing that sets us free.

Oh, dear divine, with aching soul,
Grant me the patience to let go,
The need for haste and urgent stride,
To trust the rhythm in which you guide.

For I'm weary, I confess,
Impatience lingers, causing distress,
But in this moment, I yearn to find,
The faith to surrender and unwind.

In the grand tapestry of life's design,
You weave the threads, oh power divine,
Each moment orchestrated with divine care,
In perfect timing, beyond compare.

So, grant me wisdom, dear divine,
To release the worry, to redefine,
My understanding of what's meant to be,
And trust the timing you have for me.

For in surrender, I find my ease,
A peace that grants my heart release,
With open arms, I now abide,
In the knowledge that you'll provide.

So, in this evening's sacred prayer,
I relinquish my burdens, my load to bear,
I trust in your timing, divine and true,
And surrender to the path you'll pursue.

LETTING GO

Prayer 72: Releasing Worries and Burdens

Requesting the ability to release worries, anxieties, and burdens, praying for the strength to let go of what no longer serves, and finding peace and liberation in surrender

In the quiet of this evening's embrace,
I come before you with a pleading grace,
Oh, dear divine, hear my humble plea,
Grant me strength to set my worries free.

The weight upon my shoulders so heavy,
Anxieties and burdens, they make me weary,
I yearn for release from their tight hold,
To find solace in the peace you unfold.

In the depths of my heart, I carry fears,
That consume my thoughts, drawing near,
But in this prayer, I seek your light,
To guide me through this restless night.

Grant me the courage to let go,
To release what no longer serves, I know,
For in surrender lies true liberation,
And the peace that comes with transformation.

With every breath, I release the strain,
Letting go of worries that cause me pain,
In your loving arms, I find my rest,
And in surrender, I am truly blessed.

Take my burdens, dear divine,
And let them dissipate, like the sun's decline,
May your grace wash over me like a gentle rain,
And bring me solace, again and again.

In this evening prayer, I find my release,
A moment of surrender, a moment of peace,
Thank you for hearing my heartfelt plea,
And granting me the strength to be worry-free.

LETTING GO

Prayer 73: Forgiveness and Acceptance

Praying for the willingness to forgive oneself and others, letting go of grudges and resentments, and embracing acceptance of the past and present as part of the divine plan

In this solemn hour of dusk's descent,
I come before you, my heart heavy, repent,
With pleading words, I humbly pray,
Grant me the strength to forgive today.

Oh, divine presence, hear my plea,
For the burdens of unforgiveness weigh heavily on me,
I yearn to release the shackles of my past,
And find solace in forgiveness that will forever last.

Grant me the grace to let go of resentment's hold,
To release the grudges that have taken their toll,
For in forgiveness lies liberation's key,
A balm for my wounded soul to set me free.

Help me forgive myself, for mistakes I've made,
And those I've hurt along this journey's cascade,
Grant me the compassion to accept my flaws,
And embrace the lessons learned in divine laws.

I seek the courage to mend broken ties,
To heal the wounds and let compassion arise,
With an open heart, may forgiveness flow,
And bring healing to all, both friend and foe.

In this evening prayer, I surrender my pride,
Asking for the wisdom to cast grievances aside,
For in forgiveness, I find inner peace,
A divine connection that will never cease.

May acceptance bloom within my soul's core,
Embracing the past, the present, and more,
For all is part of the grand tapestry,
Crafted by your divine hands, eternally.

Oh, merciful guide, I humbly implore,
Fill my heart with forgiveness, forevermore,
Grant me the strength to let go and mend,
In your divine grace, my wounds will transcend.

LETTING GO

Prayer 74: Surrendering Control

Praying for the strength to surrender the need for control and trust in the greater wisdom of a higher power, letting go of the need to dictate outcomes and embracing divine guidance

In the twilight's gentle embrace, I kneel and pray,
With a humble heart, these words I say,
Grant me the strength to release my tight hold,
To surrender control, as your divine plan unfolds.

Oh, heavenly guide, I plead with you tonight,
Help me let go of my desperate need to fight,
To loosen my grip on the strings I tightly cling,
And trust in your wisdom, like a bird with clipped wing.

In the depths of my soul, I acknowledge the truth,
That my desire for control is a burden, uncouth,
With trembling hands, I offer my will,
To the grander design, may it guide and fulfill.

For in the tapestry of life, I often strive,
To steer my own ship, to keep my dreams alive,
But in my quest for power, I've lost sight,
Of the beauty that blooms when I surrender my might.

So here, in this prayer, I lay down my fears,
And surrender to you, with a river of tears,
Grant me the courage to loosen my grip,
To release my control and let my spirit rip.

In the surrender, I find a solace divine,
A serenity that washes away the confines,
For you, dear guide, hold the cosmic reins,
And I trust in your wisdom, as my heart refrains.

Grant me the grace to flow with the stream,
To release my desires, like a far-off dream,
And in the letting go, may I find my peace,
As your gentle guidance brings me sweet release.

Oh, divine presence, I implore you this eve,
Teach me to surrender, to trust and believe,
In the grand tapestry of life, let me be,
A humble thread, woven by your decree.

So, I surrender my will, my desires, my all,
To your infinite wisdom, to your divine call,
Guide me, dear guide, in your loving embrace,
As I surrender control, and find boundless grace.

GRACIOUSNESS

Prayer 75: Gratitude for Kindness

Praying to express gratitude for the kindness shown by others throughout the day, acknowledging and appreciating their acts of generosity and compassion

As twilight's gentle embrace draws near,
I gather my thoughts, my voice sincere,
In humble plea, I kneel and pray,
To thank you for kindness bestowed today.

Oh, heavenly presence, hear my plea,
In gratitude, I bow to thee,
For the acts of kindness, big and small,
That touched my heart and lifted my soul.

For the stranger's smile, so warm and bright,
That brought a ray of pure delight,
For the helping hand in times of need,
That sowed the seeds of hope and creed.

For the gentle words of love and care,
That eased my burdens, my soul to bear,
For the compassion shown, without demand,
A priceless gift from a loving hand.

Oh, divine presence, I'm truly blessed,
By the kindness in this world expressed,
I plead with you, let my gratitude flow,
Like a gentle stream that continues to grow.

For the warmth of a friend's comforting embrace,
That held me tenderly in life's embrace,
For the listening ear, so patient and true,
That offered solace when I felt blue.

For the selfless acts, both seen and unseen,
That made my world more serene,
For the generosity that knows no bounds,
Creating unity where love abounds.

May my words of thanks reach far and wide,
Touching hearts with a grateful tide,
And may kindness ripple through the night,
Spreading love, compassion, and light.

GRACIOUSNESS

Prayer 76: Cultivating Grace

Seeking the ability to cultivate grace in one's thoughts,
words, and actions, praying for the strength to respond
with kindness and empathy in all situations

In this quiet hour, as twilight falls,
I come before you, my voice enthralls,
With humble plea, I bow my head,
Seeking grace, as my heart is led.

Oh, divine presence, hear my cry,
Grant me the grace to magnify,
The kindness in my thoughts and speech,
And in my actions, lessons teach.

In moments where anger seeks to rise,
Let grace prevail, and ego chastise,
Grant me the strength to respond with love,
Like a gentle dove, soaring above.

When faced with trials and conflicts deep,
May grace guide me, my soul to keep,
To see the world with compassionate eyes,
And bridge divides that oft arise.

In moments of triumph and success,
May grace humble me, and gently impress,
That all achievements are not my own,
But gifts from a higher power, unknown.

Grant me the grace to lend a hand,
To lift others up, and help them stand,
In times of need, when hearts are weary,
May my empathy and kindness be seen clearly.

Oh, heavenly presence, I humbly plea,
In your divine wisdom, shape and mold me,
Into an instrument of grace and light,
Radiating love, even in the darkest night.

May grace fill my words, gentle and kind,
And in my actions, compassion find,
Guide me, dear Lord, each step of the way,
To cultivate grace in every day.

In this evening prayer, I humbly implore,
An outpouring of grace forevermore,
Grant me the strength to follow this quest,
And in grace's embrace, I am truly blessed.

GRACIOUSNESS

Prayer 77: Forgiveness and Compassion

Requesting the capacity to forgive others and oneself,
praying for the ability to extend compassion and
understanding even in challenging circumstances

In the stillness of this evening hour,
I bow before you, humbled and sour,
With a pleading heart, I come to pray,
Seeking forgiveness at the end of day.

Oh, divine presence, hear my plea,
Grant me the grace of forgiveness, see,
For the burdens I carry within my soul,
Weigh me down and take their toll.

Grant me the strength to let go of pain,
To release the hurt, the anger, the strain,
May compassion flow from my heart,
A healing balm, a soothing art.

Help me forgive those who've done me wrong,
To let go of grudges that lingered long,
Guide me to understand their journey's plight,
And replace resentment with love's pure light.

But, dear Lord, I also ask for grace,
To forgive myself, to embrace,
The mistakes I've made along life's way,
And find compassion in my own display.

In moments when bitterness takes hold,
Let forgiveness shine, like pure gold,
May I extend compassion's gentle touch,
Even when circumstances seem too much.

Oh, divine presence, I earnestly pray,
Grant me forgiveness, both night and day,
Fill my heart with compassion's embrace,
And let forgiveness be my saving grace.

For in forgiveness, we find true peace,
A healing balm that brings release,
May I embody forgiveness' sweet art,
And let compassion reign in my heart.

In this evening prayer, I humbly plea,
Open the gates of forgiveness for me,
Grant me the capacity to understand,
And extend compassion with an outstretched hand.

GRACIOUSNESS

Prayer 78: Spreading Kindness

Praying for opportunities to spread kindness and uplift others, asking for guidance to be a source of love, support, and encouragement to those in need

In the hush of this evening's grace,
I beseech you, with tears upon my face,
Grant me the power to spread kindness wide,
To be a beacon of love, by your side.

Oh, merciful one, hear my plea,
Unveil the path for kindness in me,
For in a world that can be so cold,
Let me be a flame of warmth untold.

Guide me to see the pain and strife,
The burdens that weigh upon each life,
Grant me the wisdom to lend a hand,
To uplift others, help them to stand.

In moments when darkness looms large,
Let me be a candle, a guiding charge,
To illuminate hearts burdened with despair,
To show them that someone truly cares.

Open my eyes to the lonely and lost,
Those in need of compassion's gentle touch,
May my words bring solace and cheer,
And banish their worries, their every fear.

Grant me the strength to offer support,
To be a pillar of love, a safe port,
For those whose spirits have been torn,
Let kindness heal, like the gentlest morn.

In this evening prayer, I humbly request,
That kindness may flow, and be expressed,
Through me, a vessel of love and light,
A source of encouragement, shining bright.

Oh, divine presence, make me aware,
Of opportunities to show others I care,
Grant me the grace to spread kindness wide,
And be a beacon of love, by your side.

GRACIOUSNESS

Prayer 79: Gracious Relationships

Seeking to foster graciousness in relationships, praying for the wisdom to communicate with kindness, to listen with empathy, and to nurture harmonious connections

In the twilight's gentle embrace,
I humbly seek your guiding grace,
Grant me the strength to foster grace,
In every relationship, in every place.

Oh, hear my prayer, with a heartfelt plea,
Infuse my words with kindness, set them free,
Grant me the wisdom to communicate,
With gentleness and love, to navigate.

In the tapestry of connections we weave,
Help me to listen, to truly perceive,
Grant me the gift of empathy's ear,
To understand, to heal, to draw near.

In moments of discord and strife,
Let me choose grace to shape my life,
Grant me the patience to mend and mend,
To find common ground, to truly blend.

Guide me to sow seeds of understanding,
Nurturing bonds that are strong and expanding,
May my actions reflect harmony's song,
In every relationship, where I belong.

Grant me the humility to admit,
When I'm wrong, to make amends and commit,
To cultivate forgiveness and seek,
Reconciliation, though the path may be bleak.

In this evening prayer, I implore,
Let graciousness be the foundation we restore,
May love and respect be the pillars we raise,
In every relationship, throughout all our days.

Oh, divine presence, please bestow,
The gift of graciousness, that I may grow,
Grant me the grace to nurture connections,
And find harmony in all interactions.

CONTENTMENT

Prayer 80: Letting Go of Expectations

Seeking the ability to release expectations and desires for how things should be, praying for the grace to find contentment in accepting and embracing what unfolds

In this sacred moment, I kneel and pray,
With a plea in my heart, I humbly say,
Grant me the strength to let go and release,
All expectations that burden and cease.

Oh, divine presence, I seek your guiding hand,
To help me relinquish the need to command,
Grant me the grace to surrender and let be,
To find contentment in what's meant to be.

For often I cling to my hopes and desires,
But they become chains, fueling restless fires,
I long to find peace in accepting the flow,
And embrace the path where I'm meant to go.

Oh, grant me the wisdom to loosen my grip,
To trust in the journey, no matter how it may tip,
To release the need for control and restraint,
And find solace in the beauty of the present.

In the twilight's embrace, as the day softly fades,
I pray for the courage to let go of charades,
To release expectations, with an open heart,
And find serenity, embracing life's art.

Let me find solace in the whispers of the breeze,
In the gentle sway of the swaying trees,
May I surrender to the rhythm of life's dance,
And find freedom in each fleeting circumstance.

Oh, divine presence, I humbly implore,
Guide me to the stillness at my very core,
Grant me the grace to let go and just be,
To find contentment in life's mystery.

In this sacred moment, I release my control,
May I find peace within, and make it my goal,
To trust in the unfolding, whatever it may be,
And find joy in the journey, so graciously.

CONTENTMENT

Prayer 81: Embracing Imperfections

Requesting the strength to embrace imperfections, both within oneself and in the world, praying for the ability to find contentment in the beauty of imperfection and the lessons it brings

In the twilight's gentle glow, I kneel and pray,
With a humble voice, my plea I convey,
Grant me the strength, I beg and implore,
To embrace imperfections, forevermore.

Oh, divine presence, hear my desperate cry,
As I seek the courage to let imperfections lie,
In a world that craves flawlessness and shine,
Help me find solace in what's not divine.

For I am flawed, with scars and rough edges,
Yet within them lies wisdom that time pledges,
Grant me the grace to accept these marks,
And find beauty in the lessons they embark.

In the mirror's reflection, I often see,
The cracks and blemishes staring back at me,
Grant me the wisdom to embrace them all,
And find contentment, no matter how small.

In this imperfect world, filled with highs and lows,
I plead for the strength to let judgments go,
To see the beauty in life's asymmetry,
And cherish imperfections as a part of me.

Oh, divine presence, guide me on this quest,
To find peace in what society deems as less,
Help me embrace the imperfect, both big and small,
And learn the lessons they have to install.

In the evening's hush, I surrender my plea,
May I find acceptance and let imperfections be,
Grant me the strength to cherish the flaws I see,
And find beauty in imperfections, blessed and free.

CONTENTMENT

Prayer 82: Letting Go of Comparison

Requesting the ability to let go of comparisons and expectations, praying for the strength to find contentment in one's unique journey and to embrace one's own path without comparing it to others

As daylight fades and shadows grow deep,
I come before you, my heartache to keep,
Grant me the power to release and let go,
Comparisons that burden and sow.

Oh, divine presence, I plead and implore,
Give me strength to abandon this incessant chore,
To free my mind from the shackles of comparison,
And find contentment in my own unique version.

In a world where others' paths shine bright,
I beg for the grace to embrace my own light,
To walk my journey, unburdened by the weight,
Of expectations and comparisons that frustrate.

Grant me the wisdom to see the beauty within,
To cherish my talents and the gifts I've been given,
Help me recognize the blessings that abound,
And find contentment on this sacred ground.

For when I compare, I lose sight of my worth,
And fail to see the value of my own birth,
Guide me to a place where self-acceptance thrives,
Where comparison no longer poisons my lives.

In the stillness of this evening's embrace,
I surrender my plea, seeking your grace,
Grant me the courage to let comparison go,
And find contentment in the path I sow.

Oh, divine presence, hear my heartfelt plea,
May I release comparison and be truly free,
In the gentle twilight, I lay my prayer,
Grant me the strength to let go and to care.

CONTENTMENT

Prayer 83: Finding Joy in Simplicity

Praying for the ability to find joy and contentment in life's simple pleasures, appreciating the beauty of the present moment and the small wonders that surround us

As the day draws to a gentle close,
I kneel before you, my heart exposed,
Grant me the gift of simple joy,
In life's moments, both big and small, oh, Hoy.

Oh, gracious soul, I humbly plea,
Help me find joy in simplicity,
In the laughter of a child at play,
Or the sun's warm kiss at the end of the day.

In the gentle breeze that whispers through the trees,
Or the gentle hum of the buzzing bees,
May I find contentment in the little things,
The grace that each passing moment brings.

In the beauty of a blooming flower,
Or the quiet solitude of an evening hour,
Help me see the wonders all around,
And cherish the treasures I have found.

For in the pursuit of grand desires,
We often overlook life's humble fires,
Grant me the vision to truly see,
The joy that dwells in simplicity.

Release me from the grip of constant haste,
And let me savor life's simple taste,
In the smile of a loved one, a tender embrace,
May I find solace and abundant grace.

Oh, heavenly guide, I call upon thee,
Guide me to embrace life's simplicity,
In each passing moment, let me find,
The joy that dwells in the present, so kind.

As night descends and stars take flight,
I surrender to your divine light,
Grant me the ability to truly see,
The joy in life's simplicity.

CONTENTMENT

Prayer 84: Humility and Humbleness

Seeking the strength to embrace humility and humbleness,
recognizing that acts of grace and kindness are not about
self-importance, but about genuine care and love for others

In the quiet of this evening, I implore,
Grant me the grace of humility, I adore,
For in this world of grandeur and pride,
I yearn to let humility be my guide.

In moments of triumph, when success does gleam,
May I remember that it's not just a dream,
But a gift bestowed upon me from above,
A reminder of blessings, of boundless love.

When ego whispers, seeking to inflate,
May I find the strength to humbly negate,
To embrace humbleness, with open arms,
And let go of the need for worldly charms.

For true acts of grace are not self-serving,
But born from a heart that's truly deserving,
Of the blessings bestowed upon its core,
To share them humbly, forevermore.

Grant me the wisdom to set ego aside,
To recognize others with humility as my guide,
For in serving others, I find my worth,
In selflessness, my spirit finds rebirth.

May I learn from the lessons of the meek,
To speak with kindness, to listen and seek,
To lift others up with a gentle touch,
And let my actions speak, oh so much.

In the tapestry of life, may humility shine,
A testament of character, divine,
For it is through humbleness, I plea,
That true compassion and love shall be.

So, in the quiet of this evening hour,
I beseech you, grant me the power,
To embrace humility, with all my might,
And walk the path of love's pure light.

In humility's embrace, I humbly pray,
Grant me the strength to follow its way,
For acts of grace and kindness to discover,
And in humbleness, my soul to uncover.

CLARITY

Prayer 85: Clearing Mental Fog

Requesting the clearing of mental fog and confusion, praying for a calm and focused mind, and asking for clarity in decision-making and problem-solving

In the twilight of this weary day,
I kneel before you, I humbly pray,
Please clear the fog that clouds my mind,
Grant me clarity, answers to find.

Oh, heavenly guide, I seek your grace,
In this chaotic and bewildering space,
Release the knots that bind my thoughts,
And untangle the web that confusion wroughts.

In the depths of my soul, I yearn for light,
To guide me through this labyrinth of night,
Please grant me a calm and focused mind,
With clarity, wisdom, may I be aligned.

As the evening shadows softly creep,
Please banish the doubts that within me seep,
Illuminate my path with your divine glow,
So I may make decisions that truly flow.

Oh, bringer of clarity, I humbly implore,
Unveil the answers I'm searching for,
Grant me insight, a crystal-clear view,
To navigate life's challenges anew.

May the fog dissipate, and my mind be still,
As I surrender to your guiding will,
Grant me the gift of discernment and sight,
To find solutions with your celestial light.

In this sacred moment, I offer my plea,
For a mind unclouded, calm and free,
Guide me through the labyrinthine haze,
And lead me to clarity's peaceful embrace.

CLARITY

Prayer 86: Illuminating the Path

Requesting the illumination of the path ahead, praying for the clarity to recognize opportunities, navigate challenges, and pursue one's purpose with confidence and conviction

As the evening descends, I bow my head,
Seeking your guidance, with words unsaid,
Illuminate the path I am meant to tread,
In this prayer, my deepest desires are spread.

Oh, divine light, please shine upon my way,
In the darkness, grant me clarity, I pray,
Reveal the opportunities that lie ahead,
And fill my heart with courage, not with dread.

I yearn to see the signs that you impart,
To recognize the purpose within my heart,
Guide me through challenges that I may face,
With your wisdom, grant me strength and grace.

Illuminate the path, each twist and turn,
With your divine light, may I brightly burn,
Grant me the vision to follow my dreams,
And pursue my passions, however hard they seem.

In this plea, I surrender to your might,
As I trust in your guidance, day and night,
Lead me towards the path that's meant for me,
With unwavering faith, I embrace my destiny.

Oh, illuminator of paths, hear my plea,
In this quiet moment, I seek your decree,
Grant me the clarity to navigate with ease,
And fulfill my purpose, bringing joy and peace.

With humble gratitude, I offer this prayer,
Knowing that you'll guide me, love and care,
Illuminate my journey, my soul, my core,
Now and forevermore, I adore.

CLARITY

Prayer 87: Aligning with Authentic Self

Praying for the clarity to understand one's authentic self
and purpose, asking for the courage to live in alignment
with personal values, passions, and strengths

In the stillness of this evening hour,
I humbly bow before your power,
Grant me clarity, deep and true,
To know my authentic self, like the sky's hue.

Oh, divine presence, hear my plea,
Unveil the essence that lies within me,
Guide me to the truth, my purpose and role,
Grant me the courage to live from my soul.

In the depths of my being, I seek to find,
The path that resonates with heart and mind,
Reveal my passions, my unique voice,
So I may make a difference, rejoice.

Help me align with values strong,
To live in harmony, where I belong,
Grant me strength to break free from the mold,
Embrace my authenticity, fearless and bold.

For too long, I've wandered astray,
Lost in the expectations that led me astray,
But now I yearn for a life that's true,
To honor my calling, to be me, through and through.

In this plea, I surrender control,
And invite your wisdom to console,
Guide me on the journey to my truest self,
To live in alignment with purpose and wealth.

Grant me the courage to let go of fears,
To walk my path, shedding all veneers,
With clarity and grace, let me shine,
Embracing my authenticity, divine.

Oh, great source of wisdom and light,
Guide me through the darkness of the night,
Align my soul with the purpose I seek,
So I may live authentically, humble and meek.

With gratitude, I offer this prayer,
In the stillness of the evening air,
Grant me the wisdom to understand,
And the courage to live as I am.

SAFETY

Prayer 88: Divine Shield of Protection

Praying for a divine shield of protection to encompass and safeguard loved ones and those who are vulnerable, asking for their physical safety and emotional well-being

In the twilight's embrace, I kneel and plea,
Oh, divine presence, hear my desperate plea,
Wrap your shield of protection around the ones I hold dear,
Keep them safe and guarded, banishing every fear.

With humble words, I beseech your grace,
Envelop my loved ones in your warm embrace,
Shield their bodies from harm, illness, and pain,
Let them know love's comfort, like a gentle rain.

In this world so vast, uncertain, and cold,
I pray for their safety, a refuge to behold,
Protect their hearts from sorrow's relentless tide,
Let joy and peace within them eternally reside.

For the vulnerable souls, fragile and weak,
Extend your loving shield, the comfort they seek,
Guard them from harm, and hold them close,
Wrap them in your divine embrace, like a delicate rose.

May your shield of protection be their guiding light,
Deflecting darkness, keeping them safe in the night,
Shield their dreams, hopes, and aspirations,
Let them flourish under your divine vibrations.

Oh, sacred guardian, I humbly implore,
Surround us with your love, forevermore,
Keep us sheltered, safe within your care,
A shield of protection, a haven so rare.

With trust and faith, I surrender my plea,
Believing in your grace, I find solace and peace,
Thank you for your shield, steadfast and strong,
May it protect us all, forever and lifelong.

SAFETY

Prayer 89: Peaceful Surroundings

Requesting a peaceful and harmonious environment for loved ones and the vulnerable, praying for the removal of any negative influences or harmful situations, and inviting a sense of security and tranquility into their lives.

As twilight falls and shadows grow deep,
I come before you, my heart in need,
A humble plea I raise up to the sky,
Grant peace and harmony, oh Most High.

In this sacred hour, I humbly implore,
Create a haven of peace forevermore,
For loved ones dear and those who seek,
A refuge from turmoil, gentle and meek.

Remove the darkness, negativity, and strife,
Bring forth serenity into their life,
Banish discord and all that disturbs,
Replace it with tranquility, where love truly curbs.

May their surroundings be filled with grace,
A sanctuary where joy finds its place,
A tranquil oasis, free from distress,
A haven of solace, a respite from duress.

Shield them from chaos, worries, and fears,
Embrace their hearts, wipe away their tears,
Surround them with love, like a warm embrace,
Fill their souls with peace, a calming space.

Grant them solace in the quiet of the night,
A peaceful haven, a source of delight,
Where dreams can flourish and spirits can mend,
In an environment that nurtures, like a faithful friend.

Oh, Divine One, hear my fervent plea,
Transform their surroundings, set them free,
May peace abound, each day anew,
In the presence of love, forever true.

With gratitude, I surrender this prayer,
Trusting in your mercy, knowing you care,
Bless their lives with serenity profound,
In peaceful surroundings, may they always be found.

SAFETY

Prayer 90: Prayers for Loved Ones

Praying for the safety, well-being, and protection of family, friends, and all loved ones, asking for divine guidance and guardianship over their lives

In the quiet of this evening's embrace,
I kneel before you, seeking your grace,
With a humble heart, I utter my plea,
Protect my loved ones, oh Lord, I decree.

Wrap them in a shield of heavenly light,
Guard their every step, both day and night,
Watch over them with your vigilant eye,
Keep them safe, let no harm draw nigh.

For family and friends, near and far,
In their journeys, wherever they are,
I pray for their safety, strength, and health,
Shield them from pain, provide abundant wealth.

Guide their footsteps along the right path,
In times of darkness, shield them from wrath,
Grant them wisdom to make choices wise,
Fill their hearts with love that never dies.

Keep them from harm's way, both seen and unseen,
In every endeavor, let your presence convene,
Surround them with angels, with love's embrace,
And shower upon them your abundant grace.

Through life's trials, let them never stand alone,
Hold their hands, guide them safely home,
In moments of joy or when sorrow prevails,
May your presence comfort and never fail.

Oh, Divine Protector, hear my plea,
For those I hold dear, I beg of thee,
Keep them safe, in your loving care,
Bless them abundantly, this is my prayer.

In your mercy, I find solace and trust,
For you alone are loving and just,
With gratitude, I humbly impart,
My prayers for loved ones, held deep in my heart.

SAFETY

Prayer 91: Shielding from Harm

Praying for a protective shield against physical, emotional, and spiritual harm, seeking divine intervention to keep oneself and others safe from danger

In this hallowed hour, I kneel and pray,
With trembling voice, I humbly say,
Oh, mighty protector, I seek your aid,
Shield us from harm, don't let us fade.

Wrap us in a mantle of love and light,
Guard our souls through the darkest night,
Shield us from danger, both seen and unseen,
In your shelter, let our spirits glean.

Protect us from the perils that may befall,
Shield our bodies, let no harm appall,
From the wounds that scar, heal our pain,
Keep us safe, in your fortress we remain.

Shield our minds from thoughts of despair,
Banish anxieties, free us from every snare,
Guide our hearts on a path of peace,
Grant us solace, let worries cease.

In this world of chaos, we humbly plea,
Pour your divine grace and set us free,
Shield us from harm, both far and near,
With your mighty presence, cast out fear.

Let your shield be a sanctuary so strong,
Deflecting all that is cruel and wrong,
In your embrace, let us find refuge,
Shielded by your love, we'll never lose.

With every step we take, shield our way,
Lead us from darkness into the light of day,
In your divine protection, we shall reside,
Shielded by your love, forever by our side.

Oh, guardian of souls, hear my earnest plea,
In your mercy, let your shield set us free,
Protect us from harm, oh heavenly guide,
In your loving arms, may we always abide.

SAFETY

Prayer 92: Safety in Troubled Times

Seeking divine protection during times of uncertainty,
conflict, or natural disasters, praying for a shield of safety
and peace amidst challenging circumstances

In this hour of darkness, I kneel to pray,
Amidst troubled times, where shadows stray,
I plea for safety in this world of woe,
Divine protector, shield us, don't let us go.

When storms of uncertainty fiercely rage,
And chaos surrounds us on every page,
Wrap us in your cloak of tranquil grace,
Keep us safe, in your divine embrace.

In conflicts that tear nations apart,
Where hatred ignites and divides every heart,
I beg for peace to fill our troubled land,
Guide us with your loving, gentle hand.

When nature's wrath unleashes its might,
And disasters strike, engulfing the night,
Guard us from harm, from each raging storm,
In your shelter, let us find comfort and warm.

Oh, divine guardian, in our despair,
Grant us solace, dispel our every care,
Amidst the turmoil, be our beacon of light,
Lead us to safety, through the darkest night.

Shield us from danger, both seen and unseen,
In your protection, let us forever glean,
The peace that surpasses all understanding,
In your presence, may we find love everlasting.

Oh, source of hope, in you, we confide,
In troubled times, let us safely reside,
Guide us through challenges, both great and small,
With your shield of safety, protect us all.

RENEWAL

Prayer 93: Surrendering to Divine Presence

Praying for the surrender of the ego self and the opening of
the heart to the divine presence, seeking spiritual renewal
through a deeper connection with a higher power

In the quiet of this evening, I humbly bow,
Seeking solace and guidance, I offer my vow,
To surrender the ego's grasp, its pride and might,
And open my heart to your divine light.

Oh, gracious presence, I implore you to stay,
In the depths of my being, illuminate the way,
Release me from the chains of self and desire,
Ignite my spirit with your holy fire.

In this sacred moment, I surrender it all,
The illusions, the attachments, both big and small,
Grant me the wisdom to let go and release,
So I may find freedom, and inner peace.

Fill me with your love, your grace, your truth,
Renew my spirit, restore my youth,
In your divine presence, let me find rest,
A sanctuary within, where I am truly blessed.

Guide me through the trials, the joys, and the strife,
Lead me to the path of abundant life,
May I walk hand in hand with your eternal grace,
In every step, feeling your warm embrace.

I plead with you, dear Lord, in humble plea,
Let your presence fill my heart, set me free,
With each breath, may I feel your presence near,
And know that in surrender, I have nothing to fear.

For in letting go, I find strength and release,
A union with your love, a deep inner peace,
In surrendering to you, I find my true essence,
In your divine presence, I am filled with luminescence.

RENEWAL

Prayer 94: Cleansing and Purification

Requesting spiritual cleansing and purification, praying for the release of negative energy, thoughts, and emotions, and inviting in the renewal of positive and uplifting vibrations

In the twilight's gentle embrace, I kneel and pray,
Seeking purification on this sacred day,
Oh, divine presence, hear my heartfelt plea,
Cleanse my soul, set my spirit free.

Release the darkness that clings to my being,
Unburden me from thoughts that are demeaning,
With your grace, wash away all negativity,
And fill my heart with love's pure vitality.

I yearn for the light to dissolve my pain,
To wash away the worries that drive me insane,
Grant me the strength to let go and surrender,
To find serenity in your eternal splendor.

Strip away the layers of doubt and fear,
Let me feel your presence drawing near,
Like a river's flow, wash away my strife,
And replenish my spirit with a vibrant life.

Purify my thoughts, my words, my deeds,
From negativity's grasp, please set me free,
May your divine essence guide my way,
As I walk in purity, day by day.

In this sacred moment, I release the past,
And invite renewal that will forever last,
Let positivity fill every corner of my heart,
And from this moment on, never to depart.

With utmost humility, I surrender my will,
To your divine wisdom, I humbly kneel,
Cleanse me, oh Lord, in your loving embrace,
And grant me a spirit renewed in grace.

RENEWAL

Prayer 95: Restoring Spiritual Vitality

Requesting the rejuvenation of spiritual energy and vitality, praying for the renewal of faith, passion, and devotion in one's spiritual journey

In the stillness of this sacred night,
I humbly come before your divine light,
With a pleading heart, I seek your grace,
To restore my spiritual vitality's embrace.

My spirit feels weary, longing for revival,
In this journey, I need your guiding arrival,
Rekindle the flame that once burned bright,
Ignite my faith with your celestial light.

Renew my passion, once fervent and true,
For I've strayed from the path I once knew,
Restore my devotion, pure and unwavering,
In your presence, let my soul keep savoring.

Like a garden in need of nurturing rain,
Pour your blessings, wash away my pain,
Revitalize my spirit, like a gentle breeze,
And fill my being with abundant ease.

In this moment of surrender, I find solace,
Asking for your touch, your divine embrace,
Awaken the dormant fire within my soul,
And make me whole, once again, in your control.

Grant me the strength to overcome any strife,
To embrace my spiritual journey, vibrant and rife,
Guide me back to the path of truth and grace,
Restoring my spiritual vitality's embrace.

In your boundless love, I find sanctuary,
Revive my spirit, for I long to be free,
Renew my faith, my passion, and devotion,
In your presence, I find eternal devotion.

RENEWAL

Prayer 96: Embracing Sacred Moments

Requesting the ability to recognize and embrace sacred moments in life, praying for the renewal of awe, wonder, and gratitude for the beauty and mystery of existence

In the twilight's gentle embrace,
I come to you in solemn grace,
With a pleading heart, I humbly pray,
For the gift to embrace sacred moments today.

In the rush of life, I often forget,
To pause and see the miracles set,
Grant me the eyes to recognize,
The sacred moments that before me arise.

In nature's symphony, let me hear,
The whispers of divinity drawing near,
In the twinkling stars that adorn the night,
Let me find wonder and pure delight.

In a tender touch or heartfelt smile,
Let me glimpse the sacred for a while,
In the laughter shared with dear ones near,
Let me feel the presence of something so clear.

Renew within me the awe and gratitude,
For the beauty and mystery of existence pursued,
Open my heart to the sacred's tender call,
That I may cherish and embrace it all.

For in these moments, divine and true,
I find solace, peace, and a love that's imbued,
With a pleading voice, I ask for this plea,
To embrace the sacred, forever set free.

So let me walk this earthly plane,
With eyes wide open, not in vain,
May every breath be a sacred prayer,
And every moment, a gift beyond compare.

CONNECTION

Prayer 97: Soulful Connections

Seeking authentic and soulful connections with others,
praying for the ability to engage in heartfelt conversations,
to listen with empathy, and to foster deep connections that
nourish the spirit

In the hush of this evening's grace,
I beseech you for a sacred space,
A plea for soulful connections true,
That nourishes my spirit and my soul renew.

Grant me the gift of heartfelt conversation,
Where words flow with heartfelt elation,
May I speak and listen with empathy's embrace,
Creating connections that time cannot erase.

In the depth of another's heartfelt tale,
Let me find understanding, never to fail,
Grant me the wisdom to truly hear,
The whispered secrets of hopes and fears.

May I see beyond the masks we wear,
And find the essence we all share,
In each encounter, a chance to delve,
Into the depths of souls and hearts that swell.

For in these connections, pure and sincere,
Lies the power to heal and to draw near,
To find solace in the warmth of another's embrace,
And know that in unity, we find our grace.

So I pray, with a pleading voice so true,
For the gift of soulful connections, anew,
To engage with others in a profound way,
And create bonds that forever stay.

Grant me this, dear divine above,
To foster connections rooted in love,
And may these encounters, cherished and whole,
Nourish my spirit and make me whole.

CONNECTION

Prayer 98: Communion in Nature

Requesting a profound connection with nature, praying for
moments of awe and wonder in the natural world, and
recognizing the divine presence in the beauty of creation

In the twilight's gentle embrace,
I plead for communion with nature's grace,
Grant me moments, profound and true,
To bask in awe and wonder, through and through.

O divine spirit of earth and sky,
Open my eyes to the beauty that lies,
In every blade of grass and flower's bloom,
In the whispered breeze and birds in tune.

In the forest's embrace, let me find,
A sacred sanctuary, pure and kind,
Where the rustling leaves speak ancient lore,
And the streams sing melodies forevermore.

Grant me the gift to wander and explore,
In nature's realm, where my soul can soar,
To walk among mountains, tall and grand,
And feel the touch of the Creator's hand.

May I witness the sunset's golden blaze,
And be humbled by the moon's gentle gaze,
In the starry expanse, let me behold,
The mysteries of the universe unfold.

For in nature's tapestry, I seek,
A connection profound, a love so deep,
To feel the divine presence in every sight,
And be filled with awe, both day and night.

So I pray, with a pleading heart,
For communion with nature, to never depart,
May I be one with the earth, the sky, and sea,
And find solace and peace in their harmony.

Grant me this, O divine and true,
To be enveloped in nature's embrace, anew,
And in its beauty and wonder, may I find,
A sacred communion, forever entwined.

CONNECTION

Prayer 99: Heartfelt Relationships

Praying for meaningful and authentic connections with others, asking for the ability to cultivate deep bonds of love, understanding, and support in relationships

In the stillness of this evening hour,
I beseech thee with all my heart's power,
Grant me the gift of heartfelt connections,
Where love and understanding flow in all directions.

Oh, divine presence, hear my plea,
In the realm of relationships, guide me to see,
The beauty of souls intertwined with care,
Where compassion and empathy forever share.

May I cultivate bonds, pure and true,
That withstand the tests and trials we go through,
Grant me the wisdom to listen and understand,
To hold space for others, with an open hand.

In the depths of love's tender embrace,
Let me find solace, a sacred space,
Where hearts align and spirits unite,
In a symphony of love, burning bright.

May each word spoken be kind and sincere,
A balm to heal, to soothe, to endear,
Let forgiveness flow in abundant grace,
As we navigate life's ever-changing pace.

Grant me the strength to be present and aware,
To nurture the connections I hold dear,
To cherish and value those who stand by my side,
And offer support with arms open wide.

Oh, divine source of love and light,
Illuminate my path, guide me in this night,
May my relationships be a testament to your grace,
A reflection of your love, in every embrace.

I humbly pray for heartfelt connections to thrive,
In the tapestry of life, may love truly arrive,
Grant me this blessing, O sacred and divine,
To cultivate meaningful relationships, for all time.

CONNECTION

Prayer 100: Harmonious Interactions

Seeking harmony in interactions with others, praying for
the strength to communicate with kindness, respect, and
empathy, fostering connections that uplift and inspire

In the twilight's gentle glow I pray,
For harmonious interactions throughout the day,
Grant me, O divine, the strength to convey,
Kindness, respect, and empathy in every way.

In the tapestry of connections we weave,
Let understanding and compassion never leave,
Guide me, O sacred source, to truly perceive,
The power of words, the impact they achieve.

May my tongue be a vessel of gentle grace,
Where judgments and criticisms find no place,
Grant me the wisdom to listen and embrace,
The varied perspectives others may trace.

Oh, heavenly presence, hear my plea,
In the realms of interaction, guide me to see,
The beauty of unity, where hearts dance free,
In a symphony of love, boundless and key.

May each encounter be an opportunity,
To uplift and inspire, to create unity,
Grant me the patience to foster community,
With words and actions that radiate harmony.

As the moon rises high and stars twinkle above,
May I embody compassion, a beacon of love,
In every conversation, a gift from above,
Let harmony prevail, like a peaceful dove.

Grant me the strength to heal wounds of the past,
To mend broken bonds, to forgive and hold fast,
In harmonious interactions, may shadows be cast,
And a brighter, more unified future forecast.

I humbly pray for harmonious connections to grow,
Where kindness and empathy beautifully flow,
Grant me this blessing, O divine and just,
To foster interactions that honor and trust.

About the Author

Honor Wells is an acclaimed author and spiritual guide known for her uplifting words. With a deep understanding of the human spirit and a profound connection to the divine, she has dedicated her life to sharing transformative messages of hope, healing, and spiritual growth.

Born and raised in a small town, Honor discovered her passion for writing at an early age. She was drawn to the power of words and their ability to touch hearts and souls. As she embarked on her own spiritual journey, she felt a calling to use her gift of writing to inspire others and lead them towards a deeper connection with the divine.

Honor's exploration of various spiritual traditions and her own personal experiences have shaped her unique approach to spirituality and prayer. Drawing inspiration from ancient wisdom, she seamlessly blends timeless teachings with contemporary insights, creating a bridge between the ancient and the modern.

With a genuine heart and a compassionate spirit, Honor's words penetrate deep into the souls of her readers, offering solace, guidance, and a renewed sense of purpose. In her prayer book, "Evening Prayers: Serenity at Sunset" each prayer is crafted with meticulous care, reflecting her deep understanding of human experience and her unwavering belief in the power of prayer to transform lives.

<u>Other Prayer Books in this series</u>

Dear Reader,

We invite you to visit our website and download a FREE copy of our Daily Weekday Prayer Book, "Rays of Hope: Daily Prayers for a Brighter Week." Inside this book, you will find a treasure trove of heartfelt prayers designed to uplift your spirit, nurture your soul, and guide you through each day of the week. From Monday's expressions of gratitude to Sunday's reflections on faith and renewal, these daily prayers will help you find solace, strength, and serenity in the midst of life's challenges.

Download your FREE copy of "Rays of Hope" today and embark on a journey of spiritual growth and transformation. Let these daily prayers shine light upon your path, filling your week with hope, joy, and a renewed sense of purpose. Allow your spirit to be uplifted, your faith to be strengthened, and your heart to be filled with gratitude.

Don't miss out on this extraordinary opportunity to access a collection of prayers that will truly brighten your week. Download "Rays of Hope" now and experience the power of divine inspiration in your everyday life.

With gratitude,
Honor Wells

Scan the QR Code below to Download a FREE Copy Of "Rays of Hope: Daily Prayers for a Brighter Week."

Made in the USA
Las Vegas, NV
08 December 2024

13657507R00132